CW00536446

# Nothing too Religious

# Nothing too Religious

## Worship resources

### . . . but nothing too religious

Andrew Pratt and Marjorie Dobson

All rights reserved. In the case of hymn texts held in copyright by Stainer & Bell Ltd holders of a current Church Copyright Licensing Ltd Licence may make copies providing these are included on their returns and copyright is acknowledged. For other material for which Stainer & Bell Ltd hold the copyright, applications to copy material must be made to the copyright holder, Stainer & Bell Ltd, P.O Box 110, Victoria House, 23 Gruneisen Road, London N3 1DZ; www.stainer.co.uk. In relation to all other material local copying of readings, prayers, hymns and dramatic material for one time use in worship or study groups is allowed without further application provided no alteration is made and acknowledgment is made of authorship. Otherwise no part of this publication may be reproduced, stored in a retrieval system, or transmitted, in any form or by any means, electronic, mechanical, photocopying or otherwise, without the prior permission of the publisher, Inspire.

Copyright © Andrew Pratt and Marjorie Dobson 2008

Cover image © PureStockX

Scripture Quotations are from the New Revised Standard Version of the Bible, (Anglicized Edition) © 1989, 1995 by the Division of Christian Education of the National Council of the Churches of Christ in the United States of America. Used by permission. All rights reserved.

British Library Cataloguing in Publication data
A catalogue record for this book is available
from the British Library

ISBN 978-1-905958-20-7

First published by Inspire
4 John Wesley Road
Werrington
Peterborough PE4 6ZP

Printed and bound in Great Britain by
Printondemand-worldwide.com, Peterborough

# ACKNOWLEDGEMENTS

We would like to thank Natalie Watson who worked with us on the beginning of this collection and also Susan Hibbins who has continued with this process. We would also like to thank the other staff of mph who have been involved in the production of this book. Stainer & Bell Ltd have been helpful in providing copyright material for inclusion.

We appreciate the helpful comments of those with whom we have shared much of this material prior to publication. Last, but not least, we thank our families for their continued support.

# CONTENTS

# INTRODUCTION

We often find ourselves where we don't want to be.

'This is boring!' 'Do I have to go?'

It sounds like the complaint of a child, but we all share that experience in one way or another – and we are used to being in church.

So imagine the experience from the point of view of those who see the church and its ceremonies as archaic and irrelevant. How many people fidget through a wedding, yawn through a christening, or clearly show their disinterest in anything but their own children's performance at a Christmas service?

We who are involved in the Church have the task of at least making the experience palatable. What can we say? How can we say it? At the very lowest level, how can we catch people's attention and keep it?

We need to start where people are and take them to where we'd like them to be, rather than the other way around. We have no right to expect their attention if our worship seems totally disconnected with their everyday living. Neither can we expect them to agree with our assertive statements about God's power and authority if they have no concept of God in their lives.

So this book has been written to help people to feel at home in church on those occasions when they cannot avoid attending worship. It also offers much material that can be used away from church premises, yet it still reflects the flavour of ritual and solemnity that many situations need 'as long as it's not too religious'. The name of God has not been omitted altogether. That would be unrealistic and would totally defeat the objective of the book; many people, who would not claim to be religious, still admit to a belief in a creative power and find the idea of prayer helpful in difficult times. There are prayers, poems and meditations that can be used with individual people, as well as with groups and congregations. Sometimes the material asks awkward questions. Often it provides unconventional answers because we believe that people bring with them as much, if not more, than we can give to them. God speaks in the ways that we each need in order to be heard. Unfortunately the Church has often tried to limit those ways. Perhaps some of the pieces in this book may help us to take a wider view.

# HOW TO USE THIS BOOK

The book contains hymns, prayers, poems, complete liturgies and other material written to provide pieces that can be used just as they are, or which can be adapted, with suitable acknowledgement, for particular situations. Any item can be used individually and the liturgies and other longer items can be shortened or lengthened to suit the occasion. The book also offers ideas to take you further into your own imagination and to stimulate your own creativity.

In the case of hymn texts held in copyright by Stainer & Bell Ltd holders of a current Church Copyright Licensing Ltd Licence may make copies providing these are included on their returns and copyright is acknowledged. For other material for which Stainer & Bell Ltd hold the copyright, applications to copy material must be made to the copyright holder, Stainer & Bell Ltd, P.O Box 110, Victoria House, 23 Gruneisen Road, London N3 1DZ; www.stainer.co.uk

In relation to all other material local copying of readings, prayers, hymns and dramatic material for one time use in worship or study groups is allowed without further application provided no alteration is made and acknowledgment is made of authorship.

# I DON'T WANT TO BE HERE

Some people feel that there are times when Christian worship is inflicted on them, especially on family occasions – christenings, dedications, weddings, funerals. While adults think that they can rationalize what is happening and make allowances – they know why they're there – children gain impressions. The experience is good or bad, fun or boring. Like water dripping on stone, every drop of experience builds up memories and later, sometimes much later, a child or adult will easily see church as an option, or not, as a consequence of the sum of all these impressions. So this section tries to provide some material for times when people have to come face to face with worship in a formal setting.

## Baptism/Christening/Dedication

This hymn is a celebration of the birth of a child and could be used for a baptism, dedication or thanksgiving. Some may wish to omit verse 1.

**Gentle whisper, hardly crying**        **Hymn**

Gentle whisper, hardly crying,
downy hair and tiny nose,
hold her, sense her peaceful movement,
cuddled in her baby clothes.

Praise to God! We offer glory
for the baby that we bring;
born within our family's story,
joy will fill the song we sing.

Birth of hope, our jubilation,
child of all our dreams and plans;
here we hold love's expectation,
priceless treasure in our hands.

May we love her, and through loving
bond together, grow and learn;
then through mutual understanding
share this joy we could not earn.

8.7.8.7   Tunes: SHIPSTON or ALL FOR JESUS (Stainer)
'him' and 'his' can be substituted as appropriate.

Often the words provided for baptism and dedication services by the church contain technical language which makes no sense to the outsider. Parents and godparents are asked to make promises that they may not keep. One way round this is to encourage parents to write their own words to celebrate birth. The following ideas are offered as a prompt to this process or may simply be used as they stand.

## An order of service for baptism/dedication of a baby, within a church setting

Leader:     Why have we come today?
To link with tradition?
To tap into some form of spirituality?
To ask a blessing on this child?
To bring her/him into a safe environment?

Whether or not we can link with the traditions of the church;
whether or not we are sure that we believe in God:
whether or not this place has any significance for us;
we come here and now for the sake of this child.

This child is our special responsibility. We love her/him. We want to do all we can to keep her/him safe and protected. So we bring her/him into this place for the tradition of baptism/naming/dedication: believing that, in some way, this act will give a blessing on this child's life.

Whether or not we believe in God, God believes in us. This child, who is so special to you, is also very special to God, for whether we recognize it or not, each one of us is a unique and valued child of God.

So, as we offer this child for God's blessing, let us remember that God welcomes and blesses all children, of whatever age or state of belief.

God understands children. Jesus was born into a family home and grew up in the care of human parents. He welcomed children and said that their loving, trusting attitude was exactly what was needed for those who would follow his way in trying to change the world.

So we bring this child for God's blessing and we make promises for her/his future.

To all of you who love this child, parents, relatives, supporters and friends, we ask . . .

|          | Do you promise to love this child and to do your best to provide a safe and caring environment for her/him? |
| -------- | --- |
| **Response:** | **We promise to do that, as far as we are able.** |
| Leader: | Do you promise to help this child to develop in every way, in body, mind and spirit? |
| **Response:** | **We promise to do that, as far as we are able.** |
| Leader: | Will you remember this day as a special one? Will you explain its significance to her/him and offer the opportunity for her/him to explore that meaning for her/himself in the future? |
| **Response:** | **We promise to do that, as far as we are able.** |
| Leader: | Will those who already believe in God promise to offer support, understanding and a ready welcome to this child and to all who wish to explore issues of faith? |
| **Response:** | **We promise to do that, as far as we are able and with the help of God.** |
| Leader: | Now we bring this child for baptism/naming/dedication and to ask God's blessing on her/his life. |
|  | What name have you given this child? |
| **Parents:** | *Name/s* |
| Leader: | **EITHER:** So we baptize/name you *N* and ask for God's blessing upon your life. |
|  | **OR:** So we dedicate *N* thanking God for her/his life and asking for a blessing upon it. |
|  | *N* God blesses you and holds you.<br>May you know God's love as a reality in your life. |
|  | Let us celebrate this life and give thanks for *N*. |

*Singing, applause, handshakes, a parade around the church or whatever other action seems appropriate can follow at this point.*

# An order of service for baptism/dedication of a child able to answer for her/himself, within a church setting

All:      **O Lord our God, we thank you for our lives, and for the world in which we live.**

         **We thank you for those things that we count as blessings. On this day we thank you especially for *N* who is here because we recognize that you love her/him.**

         **We ask you, God, to give to her/him all that is good, to help her/him to learn about you, and to know of your love.**

## Promises

Leader:      I ask all of you who are gathered here: will you do everything that you can to make it easy for the children that you know to learn about God, and his Son Jesus Christ, and to grow in faith?

All:      **With God's help, we will.**

Leader:      *N*, you have asked to be baptized. Will you try to learn about God and about Jesus as you live and grow?

Child:      **With God's help, I will.**

Leader:      As parents, I ask you: will you care for this your child/daughter/son, will you love him/her, will you help him/her to learn about God, and about his Son Jesus Christ our Lord?

Parents:      **With God's help, we will.**

Leader:      As godparents, will you do all you can to help these parents in the upbringing of their child/daughter/son?

Godparents: **With God's help, we will.**

## Profession of faith

All:      **We believe in God
who created all things;
and in Jesus Christ,
who cares for us;
and in the Holy Spirit,
who helps to make us good. Amen.**

Leader:      Do you want to be baptized?

Child:      **I do.**

## The baptism

Leader:    What is your name?

*N* I baptize you in the name of the Father, and of the Son, and of the Holy Spirit.

Let us seek God's blessing for *N*.

All:    **May the Lord show you kindness and be gentle to you; may God smile for you, and give you peace.**

*The service can close at this point or, if part of an act of public worship, simply continue.*

# An order of service for dedication involving many who are not churchgoers

## Celebrating birth

*(Words in bold print are to be shared by all present. The birth of children has been celebrated by parents and families since the dawn of human communities.*

Leader:    We never possess our children.
They are individuals from before their birth.
We offer them the inheritance of our genes.
We nurture them in the light of our experience.
We bring them up in hope.
But we never possess them.

Children are born for freedom,
born to grow,
born to learn,
born to reach beyond this time,
beyond our present experience.

Today is just a time of beginnings,
a time to express our commitment
to hold and to care,
to nurture and to teach,
that one day we may let go.

Parents have/A parent has the main care of a child, but no parent should ever be alone. We are here today to signify our support and our commitment to share in the care of this child. We have a duty of care to all children with whom we have contact, and so
**We pledge ourselves to love and to nurture, to care and support, to cherish and value this child and to support *N (& N)* in her/his upbringing.**

7

Leader:     Let us claim a name for this child which is a sign that she/he is an individual, a person, in her/his own right.

Born here,
**we welcome you.**

Gift and grace,
gift to us and life to nurture.
**And so we give thanks,
and we name you N.**

We claim for you all that is worthy of humanity,
**all of which you are worthy.**

We promise to nurture you,
**to love you.**

We promise to set before you knowledge and mystery,
certainty and those things still left to fathom,
things known by fact and faith,
the things believed
and things we hold with faltering trust;
for yours is the world
and together we'll share it.
**These things we promise you.**

Come then, child, and join this happy pilgrimage,
**sing along with all of us and learn the steps of life.**

*At this point, others may greet the child or make further affirmations. A candle can be lit with the words 'May this candle signify the light to guide your path through life that you may never walk in darkness or be lost'. A cake may be cut, with the words 'We share this cake as we have committed ourselves to share in the care of N'.*

*Finally, these words may be said.*

All:     **EITHER:  We pledge ourselves to keep our promises for N.**

**OR:      We pledge ourselves to keep our promises and we
pray for God's blessing on N for now and for always.
Amen.**

# Celebrating Union

We are aware that many of the people who come to church to get married have spiritual expectations without giving expression to faith in a traditional way. They come to church because it is special or because this seems to be the right or significant thing to do. We do not believe that this is 'using the church'. The words that follow will, we hope, touch this sense of humanity struggling after God and meet the needs of those who welcome others in God's name at very special times. Same-sex blessings are still seen as controversial by many. Often churches will not allow them, and for some, this is a matter of conscience. This is not the place to debate such issues. Nevertheless some of the material that follows could be used in such circumstances. (When approriate, words required by law should be inserted within this order of service.)

## A wedding or the blessing of a partnership

**Love soars          Hymn**

Love soars where eagles cease to fly,
love sounds the grief beneath a sigh,
love never ponders how or why,
love always lives.

Love sings when silence chills the air,
love stills when chaos shatters care.
Love understands our calm despair,
love always lives.

Love enters into joy and pain,
love fills the dead with life again,
love will endure, will still remain,
love always lives.

Love joins our hearts and minds as one,
love shares our grief, our joy, our fun,
love works, love's work is never done,
love always lives.

Love offers insight to our care,
love breathes compassion through the air,
love thrives when life is foul or fair,
love always lives.

Love values colour, light and shade,
love loves the gifts that love has made,
love brightens life, will never fade,
love always lives.

8.8.8.4    Tune: ALMSGIVING (J.B. Dykes) (alternatively, a modern tune written for these words by Peter Sharrocks is available from Stainer & Bell Ltd).

Leader:      Dear *A* and *B*, we are gathered here today to celebrate your love for each other. This is a special time for you. Having found one another, and grown in understanding and love together, you now want to seek the blessing of God and the support of your friends and relatives in a public act of commitment.

              This service does not have magical properties. It will not create a relationship that does not already exist. It is a time to put down a marker, to say, 'From this day on we will go forward together, sharing all that we can, supporting each other in difficulty and loving each other in all times and in all ways.'

              It is a time for making vows and declaring intentions, and for facing the uncertainties of the future with the one thing of which you are certain: your love for one another and the hope that your love will last for ever.

## Opening prayer

Lord, our God, you have given us this day:
a day of expectation and of joy;
a day of solemnity and of happiness;
a day of certainty and of hope.
This day is a day of new beginnings.
So, loving God, we ask that you will hear our prayers, know our thoughts and enable *A* and *B* to grow in grace and love all the days of their lives.
Amen.

## Reading

*One of the following readings may be used or others selected by the participants:*
Song 1.13–17; 2.10–14; Jn. 2.1–11; 1 Cor. 13.4–13

## Statement of intent

Leader:      *A* and *B*, the Bible says that love is patient and kind, that it is not envious or boastful or arrogant or rude. It does not insist on its own way; it is not irritable or resentful; it does not rejoice in wrongdoing, but rejoices in the truth. It bears all things, believes all things, hopes all things, endures all things.
This love never ends.
Such love might seem almost unattainable, yet it is the love for which you hope.
In this light, will you *A* do all that you can to show such love to *B*?

*A:*           I will.

| | |
|---|---|
| Leader: | In this light, will you *B* do all that you can to show such love to *A*? |
| **B:** | **I will.** |

| | |
|---|---|
| Leader: | I ask you both: will you seek to learn of one another; to be patient in understanding and loving in action? Will you seek to forgive each other's failings and to build each other up in love? Will you seek to be faithful to each other today, tomorrow and forever? |
| **A & B:** | **We will.** |

## Exchange of vows

| | |
|---|---|
| Leader: | You have publicly stated your intentions and I now ask you to seal those intentions with your vows. |
| | *A*, take *B*'s hand in yours, saying after me: |

**B, I love you and as far as it is in my power, I will always love you.**
**I give you all I have and all I am.**
**I trust you and honour you.**
**When times are difficult I will stay beside you.**
**To this end I give you my life to keep.**

*B*, take *A*'s hand in yours, saying after me:

**A, I love you and as far as it is in my power, I will always love you.**
**I give you all I have and all I am.**
**I trust you and honour you.**
**When times are difficult I will stay beside you.**
**To this end I give you my life to keep.**

## Rings

*As the couple exchange rings these words are said.*

| | |
|---|---|
| Leader: | For many years rings have been a symbol of commitment. The circle of the ring never ends. And so as these rings are exchanged, we pray together: |
| All: | **We pray together that the love that *A* and *B* have for each other may be never-ending like the circle of their rings.** |

## Love is the circle      Hymn

Love is the circle that holds and enfolds,
as journeying onwards the future unfolds.
May God be our guard, our companion and friend,
may grace keep us faithful, may hope have no end.

God, give us patience to listen and learn,
to value the gifts that we never could earn.
When living is challenged and tensions are rife,
may love help us cope with the stresses of life.

God, deepen friendship and help us to find,
as one with each other, new ways to be kind;
then bind us together, bring new love to birth,
as long as we live as companions on earth.

On from this moment we go in God's grace,
we walk hand in hand filled with joy from this place;
we know in God's Spirit our lives are now bound,
in love we find heaven, let heaven resound!

10.11.11.11    Tune: SLANE

## Final prayer

Leader:      God bless *A* and *B*, we pray, as they continue on the journey of
life and love together.
May their love for each other be renewed from day to day.
May their capacity to care be refreshed from day to day.
May they always turn to each other for support and love,
confident of meeting each other's needs.
Together let us pray for *A* and *B*:

All:      **May they be friends, may they be lovers;**
**may they know care, may they know comfort.**
**May their love grow stronger day by day,**
**and may they always know fulfilment in each other's company.**
**Caring God, pour your love and joy into their lives,**
**that their love and joy may be complete.**
**In Jesus' name. Amen.**

The coming together of a couple never just affects those two people.

Here we offer some material that may be used when two people make a formal commitment to each other, or at a gathering afterwards.

### Mother of the groom

Memory and time play tricks today –
I feel my arms cradling you
at the font of baptism,
weep frustrated tears at sleepless nights,
watch delighted as your eyes,
so newly opened on this world,
widen in recognition of my face.

> But here I see you grown into a man –
> arms cradled around the woman of your choice –
> arrayed in unfamiliar elegance,
> and radiant with the newness of your vows.

Still I touch hot and grubby hands;
see grimy knees and shirt in disarray;
hear teenage tantrums, face dismissive stares
and answer endless questions.

> Time shifts again and celebrates this day.
> Take your new path with joy.
> Today, I gain a daughter through your love.
> Add new dimensions to my memories
> and look for added happiness.
> Yet, child or man, you live within my heart.
> Go with my love.

## Meant to be

'Meant to be',
you said.
Two lives
spinning
independently
through the firmament.
Cosmic aeons in preparation.
Chance collisions
in time and space.
Moulded by experience
and circumstance.

So many
possibilities …
impossibilities,
so many turnings
missed,
or taken,
bringing you to this day.
And no cliché,
or well-worn rhyme,
can formulate,
discern,
define
the beauty of your love.

'Meant to be',
you said.
'Meant to be'.

## We meet at one point

We meet at one point,
at this intersection of our days,
one moment of your lives.

And here and now,
within this place,
the image of your love
stands clear before us.

Welcomed, we witness,
sharing your joy,
sending you forward
with love and support.

May your love grow and deepen.
May you look back to this time,
this moment,
and say that it was good.

Go, then, to the rest of your life,
go together,
and go in love.

## The grain of timber

The grain of timber,
hewn and carved,
polished,
reveals a hidden beauty.
And eyes discern a pattern,
a purpose,
in quiet clouds and crashing waves,
the force of wind,
the hush of turning tide.

When once you met
you did not know what lay ahead.
Two strangers
on the threshold of discovery,
you carved and delved,
discerned and delighted
in accents of character,
gentle and fierce,
echoes of love
that others could not see.

Surprised by joy,
you found in companionship
the  friendship  that  transcends
difficulty
and delights in the other's good.

## This is your day

This is your day
The day when love,
for you,
has turned full circle.
You were conceived in love,
cherished at birth,
nurtured through childhood,
carefully supported
as you learned to face the world
in the challenging arena
of adulthood.

Now you step out together,
secure in the trust you have found,
to begin a new life of love –
and the circle turns.
Responsibility for loving
becomes your own
and the vows you share
seal your promises
to enfold this new relationship
with a deepening love.

We, who have loved you
for so long,
bless you in your loving.
Go with God,
for he is the source of our being,
the centre of your circle,
the focus of that love.

# NOTHING TOO RELIGIOUS

'God is rubbish!' This may not be the kind of language you'd use, or maybe it is. For many people, the whole idea of God doesn't make sense any more. In spite of that, from time to time, there is a nagging need to mark a special event in a significant way. It could be the necessary parting at a time of separation or divorce, the anniversary of the death of a child, or something else altogether. Even those societies that are completely secular have found a need to invent something akin to a liturgy, even if there is no mention of God. And so, for such times, we offer these resources to be used as they are and as a spur to your own creativity, when you meet with situations that we have not encountered or addressed.

## Separation and Divorce

Well before people separate or divorce there can be times of broken relationship and self-justification.

### When families are fractured

When families are fractured,
when hairline cracks appear,
when love is torn or twisted,
God heal and draw us near.

Then teach us ways of kindness,
dispel the thoughts of hate;
enable love to kindle
and anger to abate.

Renew the love that's faltered,
where understanding failed,
and draw us back together
as though love never ailed.

### God give us patience with the ones        Hymn

God give us patience with the ones
who drive us to distraction;
help us to quell the angry words
that fuel our coarse reaction.

We know that Jesus' anger stirred
confronted with injustice;
but he absorbed such violent words
and all they would accomplish.

God make us humble, help us love,
the ones we have resented,
that we might live in harmony
when hatred has relented.

8.7.8.7   Tune: DOMINUS REGIT ME

When people separate or divorce, they are often subject to real prejudice. People judge them without any idea of the true facts. There will always be those who view separation as wrong, full-stop. For the rest of us, and for those who have gone, or who are going through, that experience it is clear that parting is rarely simple or one-sided. There are occasions when there is genuine blame, when one partner has been abusive. On some occasions, when one person acts out of character and leaves home, there may be questions about how the other person was behaving to make them want to go. This does not condone desertion, but does underline the mutual responsibility of partners in breaking, as well as in forming, relationships. Both partners will have a lot of questions, will be carrying guilt or anger or both.

## Temptation

How could I have been such a fool, Lord?
It was so easy to convince myself that there was nothing wrong.
With temptation staring me in the face –
and easily identifiable –
I still gave in.

How lame my excuses were.
'If God doesn't want me to do this,
then he'll stop me.'
As if you would, Lord!
How could I not see that sometimes you make sure
we learn by our mistakes –
the hard way?
'It can't be bad, if it feels so right.'
The answer to that one is there
at the beginning of the Bible.
What else are we supposed to learn
from the story of Adam and Eve?
'No one who knows me will ever find out.'
And what happened when they did?
Shock. Disbelief. Hurt. Despair.
It took so long to put things right again.
And *you* knew all the time!

But I have learned my lesson, Lord,
and will not make *that* mistake again,
I promise.
Forgive me, please,
even though I'm finding it hard to forgive myself.
And I know that there will be new temptations
just around the corner –
and I am only human –
but keep me alert,
so that I may not fall for the plausible excuse
every time.

When breakdown comes, there is often a lot of reflection and thought, a searching for reason and looking for ways out of guilt, or towards forgiveness and even renewal.

## Lives have been broken                    Hymn

Lives have been broken. Peace has been shattered.
Words have been spoken, best left unsaid.
Lying around us, remnants of loving.
Joy out of focus, happiness dead.

Careless of feeling, we trample onwards –
barely concealing lack of concern –
hurting and bleeding follow our actions.
Where is it leading? When will we learn?

Stark and revealing, comes that dark moment,
when broken feeling makes us aware.
All we have shattered, all we have broken,
loving that mattered, no longer there.

Then comes the sorrow. Realization!
What of tomorrow? Torment, remorse!
Lord, grant us healing in our awareness,
your love revealing compassion's source.

Lord, take our sadness. Grant us renewal.
Out of this madness, help us to see,
as we rebuild life and beg forgiveness,
we find your new life setting us free.

Metre: 10.9.10.9   Tune: BUNESSAN

# After Marriage Breakdown

**Oh, God, now my marriage has ended**

Oh, God, now my marriage has ended.

It is over – and I must face the fact that vows made before you and other witnesses have been broken beyond repair.

There has been hurt and recrimination and shock and much heart-searching. There have been many tears.

But now the parting is real, and I must deal with it.

Could things have worked out differently?

Only you know that.

But I must live today – and all the tomorrows – in different circumstances now. There is so much pain, but I must move on.

Go with me, Lord, and help me to learn from this harrowing experience.

Forgive me for the part that I have played in allowing this to happen.

Show me how to deal with memories that flood my mind at unexpected
 times and bring tears, or laughter, or regrets.

Teach me to root out bitterness as if it were an invasive weed,
 otherwise it will grow and flourish and choke all positive thought
 and any chance of new growth.

Take me by the hand and lead me through the rough paths of building
 new relationships.

Touch me with your love in those desolate moments when I must learn to
 take the burden of my loneliness away from longsuffering friends.

Restore my confidence, Lord, and help me to put my life back together again.

**What will you do?**

These words might be shared one to one with another person. Or, more likely, they may be used to help you to think through what you might say. Use with care!

And now he/she has gone, what will you do? They cross the street to blame you, or to comfort and to blame him/her. They don't know how you've lived in the private corners of your lives, the adjustments and allowances, the long uncomfortable silences and the window-rattling rows. They don't know how you feel. How do you feel?

Silence can be used to enable an individual simply to be or to talk out what they feel. Then the following sentences can be used to provide an appropriate selection to frame prayer or as an inspiration for other prayers. It is important to listen so that what is offered is neither hurtful nor inappropriate.

In your guilt, may you find forgiveness.
In your anger, may you find release.
In your hurt, may you find healing.
In your loneliness, may you find companionship.
In your emptiness, may you find fulfilment.
May friends wait and listen.
May neighbours take time to understand.
May seeds of love begin to root in barren humanity.
Above all, may God hold and enfold you in the desert and lead you from the wilderness to the comfort of love.

### I am not God, I do not have

I am not God, I do not have
the power or comprehension,
the understanding of your past,
to make an intervention.

I am not God, I do not have
the depth of Christ's compassion
to recognize your inner need,
enable re-creation.

I am not God, but I have eyes
to recognize your pleading;
and I have ears, and I can hear
your words, your hope receding.

I am not God, but God will stand
by you, through pain or sorrow;
for God is here and God will love
you now, and each tomorrow.

### You know us inside out        Hymn

(based on Ps. 139)

You know us inside out,
for all our nights and days
are open to your scrutiny,
exposed to all your gaze.

Our every pulse and turn,
from long before our birth,
you held within a loving hand
to signify our worth.

Our bodies learned to grow,
we reached toward the sky,
and every bruise and scar we gained
flashed on your watchful eye.

And when we stooped and fell,
when all seemed lost and dead,
you held us when we could not hold
and took away the dread.

The apple of that eye,
so blessed within your care;
our praise will sound beyond this time
from here to who knows where.

SM    Tune: GARELOCHSIDE

And for a new start –

## As we stand before you, God

As we stand before you, God,
please help us each to see,
we can find a way that's new,
while learning to be free.

Take away the guilt that binds,
that cripples us and flaws.
Teach again your ways of grace
transcending human laws.

Touch our pain with healing grace,
then help us to forgive
and to know that we're forgiven,
now freed to love and live.

As we stand before you, God,
we're freed from all that's past;
hold us safe and help us frame
new lives of love to last.

## Two blessings for a new start

**Face the future**
Face the future,
for the past is over and gone.
Live with the memories.
Learn from experience.
Let go of grievances.
Resolve differences.
Live in the sight of God
in the way of God.
Be strong.
He has seen us through
good times and bad.
He will bless our future
as he has held our past.

**God go with you**
God go with you, wherever you go.
Each challenge he will meet with you.
In change, he will adapt with you.
Through fear, he will strengthen you.
Through doubt, he will sustain you.
In hope, he will encourage you.
In achievement, he will rejoice with you.
At each turning of life he will be
        waiting for you.
Into his care we give you.
To the end of our lives . . .

(See also Blue Christmas p.99.)

# Life's Journey

This journey begins at birth and we never know what it will bring. . .

**Infinite value is hidden, is secret**      **Hymn**
Infinite value is hidden, is secret,
held in each seed or in children we know.
Here in a husk is amazing potential,
none of us knows how a baby will grow.

Down in the earth or the warmth of a cradle,
nature is working, so quietly, unseen.
Here God will nurture the life that is sleeping,
bringing surprises we haven't foreseen.

Then in the fullness of time we discover
what love is making, and God has to share.
Here in creation and human endeavour,
grace is providing the signs of God's care.

11.10.11.10   Tune: EPIPHANY HYMN

**Coming of age**

This day marks only
a passage of time,
yet somehow grants maturity.
As you step out
into independence,
may you take with you
the love of those who have cared for you,
the guidance of those with wisdom to offer you,
the eagerness and enthusiasm of youth,
the lessons you have been taught
and those you have experienced for yourself,
and the willingness to learn
that life is unpredictable,
but that God can always be trusted . . .

whatever happens.

Birthdays, years, come and go . . .

**Another year is past, what lies ahead?      Hymn**

Another year is past, what lies ahead?
We never know, the future is untold;
but with God's grace we enter it in faith,
the years may turn but love will not grow old.

The days roll on, and nature's colours change,
the seasons move through winter, spring and fall;
the summer of our life is sometimes chilled,
but God will journey with us through it all.

So let us sing and celebrate this day
with all who share what we proclaim with joy,
that God has seen us through with boundless love
that nothing can diminish or destroy.

10.10.10.10   Tune: WOODLANDS

Age is not something to retreat from, though frailty and infirmity can sometimes make life unbearable. Yet age, at its best, brings wisdom and understanding, experience that cannot come in any other way.

**Contemplating a big 'O' birthday**

If each year is a step
equally distanced from the next,
then is it merely an illusion
that shortens the distance,
as it adds to the number?

**God, you have watched the growing**      **Hymn**

God, you have watched the growing
that brought us to this day.
Now offer us new purpose,
a satisfying way.
Now is the time for freedom,
to think of different things,
to share that special knowledge
that all our living brings.

Across the generations
we try to heal and care,
to offer human wisdom
when love is hard to share.
God, help the growth of patience
and tact in what we say,
and when the words evade us
then hear the thoughts we pray.

Now is the time to gather
what memory has kept,
and then to build new purpose
that hope can be expressed;
to grasp what God has granted,
to live a life of grace,
to demonstrate the loving
that others might embrace.

It takes a life of learning,
to make another start,
a sense of awe and wonder
an openness to art;
and then life's long reflection,
considered, crafted, weighed,
will help to give the purpose
for which we've lived and prayed.

7.6.7.6.D   Tune: AURELIA

## Time flies

Time flies. The years slip away.
Spring soon turns to winter
and the days become shorter
        in the passing.

Never-ageing God,
when we begin to count the years,
it seems impossible that so
        many have passed.
How did they slip by so quickly?
Is that birth certificate telling
        the truth?

Growing older
brings such a mixture of emotions.

Some days there is great joy
in the wisdom of experience
and the bank of memories
that we have stored to carry
        with us.
Some days we are determined
to enjoy life to the full,
to find new challenges
and new places,
to expand our horizons.

Some days the muscles ache,
the joints creak,
movement is an effort,
and ageing is a curse.
Some days we turn to thoughts
we would rather not consider.
How many tomorrows?
How will we cope?
What might we miss?
And the future is too disturbing
to contemplate.

Loving God,
hold us in our darker days
and lift our spirits and keep us safe
when troubles are around us.
Comfort and heal
in times of ill-health, or sorrow.
Calm our fears in times of anxiety.
And keep us looking forward,
living life as fully as we are able to
and meeting each new day with hope
as we know that you are with us
and surrounding us with your
        love and care.

## Is there a point?

Is there a point
when the years ahead
seem fewer than those behind;
when death
becomes, strangely,
more significant
than the birth we have celebrated?

**God marks no ending, only new beginnings**     **Hymn**

God marks no ending, only new beginnings,
until the consummation of our lives;
God keeps no count of losses, nor of winnings:
we move through grace, the Holy Spirit thrives.

So as we go beyond this time, this setting,
rememb'ring all the laughter and the tears;
we go with God in faith, so not regretting
the moments shared, the hopes, the dreams, the fears.

Though parted for a while, we travel onward,
not knowing what the future has in store.
This phase will close, the Spirit draws us forward,
we've tasted love, but God has promised more!

11.10.11.10   Tunes: LORD OF THE YEARS or PERFECT LOVE

# Losing a pet

For some people animals are close companions. I have a friend who did a lot of walking – many, many miles. His dog walked with him. When the dog died he really grieved. For children the death of a pet may be the first death they experience. This time the 'sleep' is permanent. And so for the death of a pet:

**This animal has shared our lives**

This animal has shared our lives
has lived through many seasons;
and though it may seem strange to some,
we grieve, we have our reasons.

Theology has sometimes stressed
our human domination;
biology would see us all
as part of one creation.

This planet has been lent to us,
with every striking feature;
and we are stewards of this earth
to care for every creature.

And so we offer thanks to God,
for loss that is revealing;
an insight into love and grace,
for common life and feeling.

# Death and Dying

Within this section there are items for funerals and for memorial services. For more extensive material related to death and bereavement please see *Poppies and Snowdrops* (Andrew Pratt and Marjorie Dobson, Peterborough, Inspire, 2006). The following hymn appeared in that book but this version has been revised to take account of the fact that, increasingly, younger people are grieving for friends killed in global conflicts. Others are living with various disabilities and memories that will affect the rest of their lives.

**By a monument of marble**    **Hymn**

By a monument of marble,
or by simple wooden cross,
here we gather to remember
sacrifice and tragic loss.
Blood-red poppy petals flutter,
each a symbol for a life,
drifting in a crimson curtain,
shadow of our constant strife.

Solemn silence now surrounds us
as we stand in memory.
Why should evil lead to conflict?
This eternal mystery
troubles hearts and stirs the conscience,
urges us to think again;
face the curse of confrontation,
yet reduce this searing pain.

For the sound of war still thunders
through our planet, on this day.
Every hour new victims suffer,
even as we meet to pray.
God, beyond our understanding,
peace seems far beyond our reach;
move us on to new solutions
through that active love you teach.

8.7.8.7.D    Tune: LUX EOI

Year on year we still remember, and need to remember, the Holocaust, the period during the Second World War when millions of Jews and others were systematically killed by the Nazis. We remember because this devastation could be repeated. It was planned and executed by human beings and we are human. The text could be used on Holocaust Memorial Day, 27 January, the anniversary of the liberation of Auschwitz, one of the concentration camps where people were taken, ostensibly to work, but where many thousands were exterminated.

### As we remember holocaust    Hymn

As we remember holocaust,
in penitence, we pray;
for death that we commemorate
can come again today.

The world still offers evidence
of hate in human hearts,
continued inhumanity
when human love departs.

And we confess again, O God,
that in us grow the seeds
of hatred and derisive fear,
that here compassion bleeds.

So now we kneel in prayer again,
the many and the few,
forgive us when we turn aside
from duties we should do.

O source of sacrificial love,
in penitence, we pray:
renew our love, bring people hope,
in this and every day.

CM    Tune: ST COLUMBA

## An order of service for a funeral

Leader:  What can we say? For all of us life has its beginning and its ending. This is all part of human experience. It is so normal. Yet this is not normal at all. We are here because *N* has died. No beautiful and solemn words can take away that fact. Yet we look to one another for support and hold on to whatever faith or hope we have as best we can.

**God, as we gather in this place**       **Hymn**

God, as we gather in this place,
where thanks are mixed with tears,
we need your help to face this day
and grace to calm our fears.

No pretty words can take away
the emptiness we feel,
for grief is raw and faith is frail,
and death is very real.

So help us to accept the truth
of all we have to bear,
to cope with this reality
within your love and care.

CM   Tune: LLOYD

Leader:  This time is for remembering, for sharing, for supporting each other in love.

It is a time to begin learning to live with the reality of what has happened. Paradoxically, then, it is a time for looking forward.

Let us pray:
God, we come to you in different ways.
Some of us are filled with hope and strong in faith;
some have had their strong faith shaken if not destroyed;
some come to you as a last resort,
hoping against hope that comfort might be found here,
a way forward out of the bleakness of this moment;
for some of us all this is so much mumbo-jumbo,
a ritual to pass through on the way to the grave, that makes little contact with the reality we know and experience.
However we come to this moment, we ask you God, to meet our need, to enable us to give our thanks for *N* and to be comforted.

Hold us always in your love and enable us, as we receive your care, to comfort one another. **Amen.**

For Christians, the Bible has always been a source of comfort and of inspiration, yet at moments like these it can seem empty and hollow, even hurtful. With that awareness we share these words:

## Reading
*A reading from one of the following or another suitable passage:*
Ps. 23 and/or 121; Lk. 12.22–28; Rom 8.35–39.

## The tribute
*This is a time to share memories of the person who has died. More often than not they will have been gathered beforehand and one person will share them on the day. Sometimes family members will appreciate the opportunity to do this. On some occasions, when people have been prepared before the service, individuals from the congregation could share recollections very briefly, so a spoken montage could be built up to focus thought and memory.*

## Prayers
*Extempore prayers, based around these recollections of the deceased, may be offered. In addition, or instead, the following prayers may be used:*

We thank you, O God, for N whom we have cherished and remembered. He/she has changed our lives by things he/she has said and done and by the ways in which we have related to him/her.

Thank you for all those special characteristics which made him/her different and unique. We are grateful for particular memories and intimate moments that we have shared.

We ask that you will hold him/her and us ever in your love. **Amen.**

As people bound by our friendship and relationship to N, we ask that you will forgive us for any times that we may have failed or hurt him/her. Release us from any sense of guilt or regret. Absorb any anger we may feel.

Relieve any sense of hopelessness that we may experience. Strengthen us in our weakness and comfort us in our distress.

May smiles of gratitude and the warmth of laughter be rekindled in our lives as we remember happy times we have spent together.

Help us to enter the future knowing that we have been immeasurably enriched through our relationship with him/her. Receive our thanks for his/her life and shield us with your love, now and evermore. **Amen.**

*If the Committal is to take place as part of the service it will do so at this point. Otherwise it will take place separately before or after the main service above.*

Leader:     We acknowledge that *N* is held in God's love. Some will name this heaven. We affirm that *N* is safe whatever has gone before this moment. So all that we say is framed in this light.

O God, we ask you to continue to care for *N* whose mortal remains we now lay to rest.
*At this point the coffin is laid in the earth or, in the crematorium, lowered or shielded by curtains as desired.*

God receives our thanks, hears our prayers and enfolds us in love. **Amen.**

### Stay with your people through aeons of sadness          Hymn

Stay with your people through aeons of sadness,
nights that seems endless, when hope seems to fail.
Go with us, God, with your calm understanding,
nurturing gracefully faith that is frail.

Go with us, God, to the future that beckons,
dawn that is distant, where day will not break.
Go with us, God, where your grace can awaken
love that is constant, that grief cannot shake.

Go with us, God, may your love never leave us,
though dark enfolds us your love is our light.
Stay with your people and never forsake us,
till dawn's new colour brings hope to our sight.

11.10.11.10    Tune: STEWARDSHIP, WAS LEBET, STREETS OF LAREDO

As we return to the duties and tasks of our lives, may God go with us and may we support and encourage each other for the rest of our days.
We ask it in Jesus' name. **Amen.**

Christians believe in life before, but also beyond, death:

### Here on the crest of the wave of creation      **Hymn**

Here on the crest of the wave of creation,
roaring and rolling beyond time and place;
God is transforming through quiet resurrection,
challenging hopelessness, offering grace.

Now we will follow the steps that will lead us
on through the horrors and hatred of life,
on through the angst-ridden pain of bereavement,
on through the cross to the ending of strife.

Here at faith's edge where our peace is beginning,
God soaring free through our chaos and pain,
here is the meaning of loving and living,
here is the place of our rising again.

11.10.11.10   Tune: SPEAN

### For the anniversary of a death

Loving God, we come to you today because it is the anniversary of the day that *N* died.

This day is full of emotion. Sadness, because of the gap left in our lives when she/he died, and memories, some very painful, some full of joy.

We remember the good times, and the times that were not so good. There was laughter and love to share, but there were also stressful hours when patience was tried, tempers frayed and life was not easy.

We thank you for *N* and for the privilege of being a part of her/his life.

As the years pass and life changes, help us to move on to the future with hope, even though we will never forget that *N* played a significant role in our lives.

Compassionate God, bless our memories and lead us gently through this special day. **Amen.**

# WHAT ON EARTH ARE YOU ON ABOUT?

## People and Politics

The words that we hear in church are increasingly irrelevant. It is possible to argue that impenetrable language adds to mystery and, perhaps, sometimes it does. More often it confuses. Even when what we say is understood, it often seems far removed from our day-to-day experience of life and of the world in which we live. Simply looking around our towns and cities we can see evidence of themes and questions which are remote from the agenda of our churches. Nevertheless these are issues that we should try to address.

The council offices or town hall might be our starting place. Political activity often operates at a local level and in a religious, if not Christian, context. These words were written for the service of induction of a mayor:

**Our civic duty we will share**     **Hymn**

Our civic duty we will share,
whatever politics or creed:
to serve our neighbours as ourselves,
to foster peace through word and deed.

To work together under God,
release potential, channel grace,
to offer value, show respect,
to every person, every face.

Whatever trial may come our way,
God, help us show integrity,
as working for a better world
we strive to seek equality.

We share a task of common care,
of service in community,
we meet to dedicate ourselves,
to demonstrate our unity.

LM   Tune: CHURCH TRIUMPHANT

## Our responsibility

Another banner headline screams out against politicians, local or national, and we unite against the common enemy, totally critical of the actions taken by those we have elected to power. Is this always right?

**Dear God, how do we get the balance right?**

Dear God, how do we get the balance right?
How do we exercise the right to question the decisions our politicians make, yet at the same time have understanding about the complexity of their work and the stresses and demands that are placed upon them?

How do we defend democracy and the right to representation of all views, yet at the same time fight against the injustices that the system can bring?

Wise and loving God, help us to have more awareness and understanding in our response to the authority of government, at all levels of office.

Challenge us to play an active part in the decision-making process by voting wisely; by supporting and questioning those in authority; by being prepared to make our voices heard when we believe that unjust decisions have been made and by being prepared to face the challenge of personal involvement, if that proves to be the only way of bringing about change.

There are those who tell us that politics are nothing to do with faith, but Jesus criticized the corrupt authorities of his day and demonstrated that all people are equally loved by God and deserve respect and care.
Teach us to look through your eyes and to see the needs of others, daring us to respond in action. Help us to continue the process of challenge and change that will work to make communities and a world built upon the principles that Jesus taught.
For your world's sake. **Amen.**

The world in which we live is home to many cultures and religions. Often they compete for money, status or converts. Somehow we need to find ways of co-existing which offer more than just tolerance.

Faithworks (www.faithworks.info/) is the name of an organization in the United Kingdom that seeks to enable the outworking of principles of faith, and not just Christian faith, in local communities and contexts.

**Faith works, but how can love be shown**      **Hymn**

Faith works, but how can love be shown
within a world of complex care?
Between each nation, in each town
how can God's love be focused there?

A different language, creed or dress
can build a wall and damage life;
and ignorance or fear of faith
could break our trust and fire our strife.

How can we legislate for peace,
or work for human harmony,
within a world of disparate needs,
maintaining our identity?

God, give us confidence to see
your face in people all around
that, in a world of many faiths,
your seeds of love may find rich ground.

LM    Tune: MELCOMBE

## Wise and loving God

Wise and loving God –
where prejudice makes cruel conduct blind –
open hooded eyes to your truth.
Where condemnation is deaf to alternatives –
make your inner voice heard.
Where bigotry shuns contact –
show the power of your loving touch.
And wherever people are hurting –
make them aware of the depth of your compassion –
and of your ability to transform broken lives,
for your understanding love
is often their only hope
in an unfeeling world.

The story of the Good Samaritan points to the reality that our neighbour can
be anyone. This is such a familiar story that preachers almost feel a need to
apologize for using it . . .

## Not that again!

A.    Oh no! Not the Good Samaritan again! I don't believe it!

B.    You mean you don't believe the story of the Good Samaritan? It's one
of the most favourite ones in the whole Bible.

A.    Of course I believe in the story – it's just that we never seem to hear
the end of it.

B.    Oh, I know what the ending is. The Samaritan takes the wounded man
to an inn and . . .

A.   Oh, come on! I didn't mean I didn't know the ending of the story, I meant that we keep hearing the whole thing over and over again.

B.   But it's good, isn't it? I mean, it's got everything. Mugging, passers-by who couldn't care less, and the character you least expect to be the hero turns up trumps. What more could you want?

A.   What I want is a change of story.

B.   You mean turning it round so that the Samaritan really turns out to be the villain after all and finishes the job that the robbers left and murders him?

A.   No, you fool! I don't mean that at all . . . although that idea does have possibilities.
     What I mean is that I'm just heartily sick of hearing the story yet again. You know why she's doing it, don't you?

B.   No. But I'll bet you're going to tell me.

A.   It's obviously her favourite sermon, isn't it? I mean, all preachers have a favourite text, or a story they've preached about for years. This'll be hers. You can guarantee that this sermon will be as old as the hills and she'll have preached it in every church she's ever visited.

B.   Oh, come on! Be fair. It's a great story and there are loads of variations of it.

A.   I know! I know! I've heard loads of versions as well.

B.   There was one where the characters are a social worker, a minister and a local councillor and the hero was a punk rocker . . .

A.   I know! I know!

B.   . . . and another where the hero was a new-age traveller . . .

A.   Yes, all right!

B.   . . . and another where the bloke drove a Merc, the first person to stop was in a Land Rover and the Good Samaritan didn't turn up at all!

A.   What are you on about? How can you have a story about the Good Samaritan if he doesn't even turn up?

B.   Well, at least it's original!

A.   Which is more than this sermon's going to be! I suppose we'd better let her get on with it. Come on then, woman – tell me something I don't know!

B.   Why should she bother to do that? It won't make any difference to you. You can't hear her when you're sleeping anyway!

The words can lead to the sermon, or maybe just a quiet reflection: 'Well, you know who your neighbour is, and you know Jesus said to love your neighbour. Go on then.'

And a hymn and a prayer . . .

## We cannot make an easy, safe distinction          Hymn

We cannot make an easy, safe distinction,
all people are our neighbours, none denied;
the voices of all nations heard beside us:
all sisters, brothers, none we should deride.

The wall between the peoples has been broken,
in love of God divisions disappear;
as seen in Christ we recognize our neighbours
We greet unusual faces without fear.

We celebrate each difference God has given;
each nation, black and white, both straight and gay;
the able and the challenged God has offered
that we might share together, learn and pray.

We meet with those who paint a different picture,
who value God in words not yet our own,
in dialogue we offer one another
a vision we could never find alone.

This God we seek is greater than each difference,
the source and ground of all variety,
the centre and the soul of all creation,
erasing hate with love to set us free.

11.10.11.10   Tune: INTERCESSOR

## Forgiving God

Forgiving God,
we come to you
with memories of things which have divided us in the past.
Sometimes these misunderstandings
were based on things that happened long ago
and have been handed down as fully-fledged prejudices.
Sometimes we have been so involved in our own way of doing things
that we have considered any other way to be irrelevant.
Forgive us,
renew us
and give us the courage to think again. **Amen.**

Political actions affect the way we treat people. How well we treat those least valued by our community is a sign of the depth of our humanity.

**Being moved is not enough**

Being moved is not enough,
sentiment will not persuade
the hated and the world's despised
that love has met their need.

Action more than any words
demonstrates that we have heard
the cry of Jesus, Jesus' pain,
embodied in this time.

Once they left him hanging there,
crown of thorns and nails of iron,
hard hammered to that cross of wood,
they left him there to die.

Blood was on their hands, and ours,
leaving people in their need,
and only when we turn to love
is life renewed, redeemed.

Altruism is sometimes necessary though difficult to achieve. When we are confronted by a crisis we often see religious and political labels put aside. What matters then is our common humanity. Here we really begin to love our neighbours as ourselves.

**In times of crisis when we act**          **Hymn**

In times of crisis when we act
without a thought of self, or fear;
when all that matters is the love
that meets another's crying need,
the love of God prevails, draws near,
and grace makes each relation clear.

To Muslim, Christian, young or old,*
we reach with hands of boundless hope;
not knowing where to find the strength,
we struggle through discord, distrust,
with God's unbound resource we cope
and offer love of greater scope.

We circle all the world with care,
the dance and song are intertwined,
the proud gavotte, the tango's pulse,
the lieder's warp, the ballad's weft,
conjoined with God we're wined and dined,
our love made pure, now unconfined.

88.88.88   Tune: ABINGDON
*This line may read: 'To all God's people, young or old'

## Can we care enough?

Can we care enough?
How can we really know the depths
of someone else's need?
How do we identify
with someone who has nothing at all,
while we demand basic comforts
from the state,
as a matter of course?
And get them.

Compassionate God,
open our blinkered eyes
to see the real world of need.
Take us out of our comfort zone.
Make us blind to difference,
open to variety
and touch sensitive.
Help us to see,
not just a faraway problem
unrelated to our daily lives,
but other human beings,
with needs and hopes like ours.

And as you wake us up
to the reality of compassion,
stir us to begin
to answer our own prayers
in very practical
and self-giving ways.

For your world's
and our neighbours' sake.
**Amen.**

When love is foremost we meet each other's needs.

**There is no clash of creeds**          **Hymn**

There is no clash of creeds,
no hatred thought or said,
where love is taken seriously,
where neighbour's needs are fed.

Beliefs are put aside,
so care can take the stage;
no creed is more important here
than loving come of age.

The gamble that we take
from each religious frame,
is letting go of certainty,
of silencing our claim.

No pride in rite or creed
is ever worth a life;
for this humanity we share
transcends all human strife.

Together let us build,
and keep the end in view:
a vast community of love
for all, not just the few.

SM    Tunes: SANDYS or GARELOCHSIDE

One day, perhaps, we'll find the unity that at the moment seems to be the stuff of dreams.

# Natural Disasters

The challenges that face us in the world are not just brought about by human action. Natural disasters afflict us and often have worldwide consequences.

Time and again our understanding of the world and, if we have a religious belief, of God is challenged by experience. We see news of floods, tsunamis, earthquakes; so many things which force us to ask the questions: 'Why does God allow this?' Where is God in all of this?

Our worship cannot duck these questions or answer them with simplistic platitudes. We may not have all the solutions, but we ought at least to communicate clearly those things we do know, of which we are sure. As to the rest, our admission of agnosticism should be just as honest and transparent.

Here are some thoughts to spur you in your own exploration of evil and what it says of God. To begin with, some words written in response to a mud slide:

## All hope has slid with casual inhumanity

All hope has slid with casual inhumanity,
a sea of mud, an agonizing sigh;
and those who seek to meet in this catastrophe
the face of Christ will hang their heads and cry.

A natural phase, or consequence of thoughtlessness,
the fruit of greed that had a human cause;
or 'acts of God' that magnify our carelessness?
These visions challenge grace, prompt faith to pause.

But God is here with love beyond imagining,
the spirit of relief that looks for life;
the pleading human groans within the damaging,
the spark of hope that penetrates our strife.


## It's happened again

It's happened again, God!
Why, God? Why?
Why don't you stop these things before they get out of hand?
If you are the creator that you claim to be, then why do you allow such disasters to happen?
They destroy your creation and take the lives of your people as well.

You are supposed to be a loving God.
What's so loving about destruction?
What's loving about so many people being injured, or dying?
How can there be any good in any of that?

O God, we are totally bewildered by disastrous events and devastated by the thought of so much loss of life.
Help us, as we struggle to take it all in.

Teach us how to show practical compassion in our efforts to help those who have lost everything.
Encourage the rescue workers and emergency services and show us the best way to offer our support.
If there are lessons to be learned that may prevent the same thing from happening in the future, then guide us in the positive steps that have to be taken.

God, we do not understand why, but we want to do our best to make sure that it doesn't happen again.
Absorb our anger and transform it into action. **Amen.**

There has been a tendency within the church to see only good within creation. Only the good things we see are attributable to God. Bad things are ignored or attributed to the 'work of the devil'. But if God means GOD then that's where the buck stops:

### Deep contradictions, not cosy solutions     **Hymn**

Deep contradictions, not cosy solutions,
come when our faith and experience collide.
Pain and its purpose, the holocaust's image,
loving and hurting, are found side by side.

Here in the tension of unresolved conflict,
logic and passion will vie for each heart;
here in life's crucible, melting and moulding,
God has a purpose and we play a part.

Here where the Spirit is forging, transforming
lives that are open to challenge and change;
God in each paradox fathoms potential,
source of the pattern we measure and range.

11.10.11.10    Tune: EPIPHANY HYMN

The jury is still out on the degree to which the climate changes we are witnessing are part of a cycle of change working over millennia and the extent to which human action affects these changes. One thing is sure, wherever we go as human beings we affect and change the environment we inhabit, sometimes in minute ways and often with greater consequences.

### The footprints where your people tread     **Hymn**

The footprints where your people tread
have marked and marred the earth.
The global warming that we dread
has shadowed us from birth.

As climates change and nature shifts,
we play a godless game.
We reap rewards from what we sow,
yet try to shift the blame.

O gracious God, we pray for help,
that we might learn to live
in harmony within this world
with all you gave and give.

CM    Tune: KILMARNOCK

[Jesus said,] 'Truly I tell you, just as you did it to one of the least of these who are members of my family, you did it to me' (Matthew 25.40 NRSV). So what we do today and how we relate to each other indicate both our closeness to God and the level of our responsibility for our own actions. How we treat the world and how we respond to each other will have consequences beyond the present moment of our actions.

### Terrors and ecstasies lurk in creation      Hymn

Terrors and ecstasies lurk in creation;
loving and laughing, and torture and fear;
all human knowledge can offer an insight
into the cosmos God treasures, holds dear.

Not in the abstract, but here in the present,
things we are doing and things left undone,
scourge and berate Christ, we crucify Jesus,
here in our choices is God lost or won.

Look to the present, the people sat near you,
ones you would honour and those you despise;
justice you speak of when lived and enacted
brings life to people, God's love is our prize!

11.10.11.10   Tune: STEWARDSHIP

# I WANT TO FIND OUT ABOUT
# SPIRITUAL THINGS (1)

Many people seek their spirituality outside the Church. A number of the disciplines or activities that they follow include meditation techniques and inner reflection. They may not call this activity 'prayer', and they might disregard what the Church has to offer as being too full of words and too ritualistic and formal.

In order to reach these seekers for truth, it may well be necessary for us to rediscover some of the quieter forms of meditation that have always been a part of the spiritual life of many Christians.

So here we offer ideas for spiritual journeys, not necessarily inside the church building. Labyrinths, Quiet Days and Pilgrim Walks are a few of the ways in which creative connections can be made with those looking for a deeper meaning to life.

## Labyrinth

The labyrinth experience is a journey towards God, letting go of stress and conflict; a meeting with God at the centre; and a journey out to appreciate the creative power and the challenges that are in store for us when we follow God's way.

All this is contained within a path, based on patterns set by the medieval cathedral mazes and surrounded by sights, sounds and scents to inspire reflection and thought. Many of these labyrinths are based on ancient designs and can be used inside or outside a building. But each labyrinth works best when it is adapted to its particular setting. Some types of labyrinth could be classed as guided prayer walks, but the name is immaterial. What is important is the experience of touching a deeper vein of spirituality; one that is also open to those who would not be comfortable with attending conventional church worship.

Information about labyrinths based on cathedral patterns is available through groups especially dedicated to that art. But labyrinths themed and adapted to events, or particular buildings, can be as adventurous and inventive as the planners who conceive them. The example given here was set up in a large room in part of the Spa Complex in Scarborough, North Yorkshire, for an Easter People event. The room had the advantage of a sea view from one end, so that was used for one of the reflective stages. Masking tape marked out the paths guiding people around the room – this tape sticks to anything (even the new carpet that had only been laid days before the event!) but is easily and cleanly removed afterwards.

There were six stages of reflection, plus an entrance display and a significant exit. The equipment needed was fairly simple and readily available, although any local specialist skills should be used to make the displays as helpful and as striking as possible. The theme was 'The Journey to Freedom' and each stage reflected on some aspect of this subject. Quotations and brief texts were placed on cards at strategic points along the way.

The stages were planned and equipped in the following way.

## Entrance

*Equipment needed – full-length free-standing mirror, chains of all shapes and sizes, suitable quotations on card.*

The free-standing mirror was criss-crossed with the chains, so that as people looked at their reflection they saw themselves in chains. Various quotations were placed around, including Charles Dickens, from 'A Christmas Carol': 'These are the chains I forged in life!'

## First stage

*Equipment needed – rolls of plain paper (lining paper is ideal), thick felt tip pens for drawing chains, shredder, waste bins, self-adhesive notes, note pads, pens, chairs.*

The lining paper was fastened to the wall in long rows and chains were drawn on it in large links with thick black pen. The other items were available on tables, as needed.

## Second stage

*Equipment needed – small hand mirrors, boxes of tissues, waste bins, chairs.*

Chairs were set out in a rough circle with enough space between to give privacy, bins were placed in the centre and mirrors and tissues on a nearby table.

## Third stage

*Equipment needed – as large a free-standing cross as the area will take, several metres of red fabric, nails, chains, banner proclaiming 'he breaks the power of cancelled sin, he sets the prisoner free', holding crosses, floor cushions, chairs.*

The large wooden cross was draped with the red fabric, so that the fabric flowed down and around the foot of it. Nails and chains were scattered around and on this fabric and alongside the banner. Small wooden holding crosses were within easy reach and floor cushions and chairs were provided.

### Fourth stage

*Equipment needed – cut paper strips for paper chains, pens, cards printed with 'fellowship', 'faith', 'caring' and other positive words.*

Paper links and pens were provided on the table that also held the growing paper chain, and cards were placed on the wall behind.

### Fifth stage

*Equipment needed – leaflets from Amnesty International, Release and any other suitable organization. Pictures and memorabilia, if possible, of those persecuted for their beliefs.*

Mock up a prison cell, as inventively as possible. The leaflets should be accessible to read and, if possible, have enough copies so that they can be taken away if people want to take action after they have prayed.

### Sixth stage

*Equipment needed – deck-chairs or garden chairs, challenging texts, bowl, coloured paper clips.*

Deck-chairs were placed to look out at the sea view and the horizon. If there is no view, then a world map, pictures of wide skies and clouds, or landscape paintings or photographs could be used to give the illusion of looking outside. Bowl with paper clips was placed at the exit point of this stage.

### Exit

*Equipment needed – banner with 'My chains fell off, my heart was free. I rose, went forth and followed . . .'*

Try to leave by a different door to the entrance, if possible, but the banner should be placed prominently over the exit.

*Also needed – text for guide cards, laminate sheets, bin liners, masking tape, CD player and discs (optional – some people appreciated quiet reflective sound effects, such as music with birdsong or running water – as a background to meditation. There were one or two who felt that this was not helpful).*

Some labyrinths give instructions with audio guides. That is good, but is often too expensive to set up. We found that simple instructions for each stage, printed and then laminated, could be used again and again and also helped people to concentrate on the experience. Several large-print copies were made for those with sight impairment. Each person was handed a guide card at the entrance door and advised to read a stage at a time. The text for this labyrinth is given below.

## Journey to Freedom – the Labyrinth

You are on a journey to freedom. Take time to look and reflect at each stage of the way.

This journey is a very personal one – no one else will experience this in exactly the way you do. It is your individual walk with God.

### Entrance – Reflection

Look into the mirror, you see yourself in chains.

Remember Marley's ghost from Dickens' 'A Christmas Carol'? He told Ebenezer Scrooge, 'These are the chains I forged in life!' His chains were money, possessions and greed.

What chains are beginning to weigh you down? Are you making them for yourself?

### First stage – Freedom from the past

Pick up a piece of paper, a pen and a self-adhesive note. Sit and reflect upon the past. Is there a time, date, place, person or situation in your past that is chaining you down? Do you need to resolve that with God? Think and pray about it. On the self-adhesive note write a date, or name, or whatever is significant. Stick this to one of the links in the chain display. On the paper, write down what is troubling you, talk to God about it and then shred or bin your paper, as a sign that God is dealing with it, with you.

### Second stage – Freedom in the present

Pick up a hand mirror and a tissue. As you reflect your face in the mirror, is there something today that you need to resolve with God? A calling you've not answered? A challenge not taken up? Something wrong that you've not put right? A personal temptation holding you back? A lack of faith? A question to ask God? Touch your face in the mirror. Remember God knows that face even better than you do. As you reflect and think, you make finger marks on the mirror. Wipe off those marks with the tissue, make a clean start with God, put the tissue in the bin and move on.

### Third stage – Freedom for the future

Here is a central cross. Reflect and remember that Jesus died there to show that God's love has no limits. Pray about your own personal chains and what this freedom will do to your life. There are holding crosses which some people find helpful in prayer.

### Fourth stage – Freedom to build a new future

Some links are good ones – fellowship, faith, caring, sharing, compassion. There are actions each one of us can take to create those links. Join into this chain by writing your name on a link and adding it. The chain is fragile, but can keep on growing if everyone joins into a positive chain of action.

### Fifth stage – Freedom for others

This is where we remember those who are imprisoned for their faith and pray for them. Here are reminders of the chains and bars that physically prevent these people from practising their faith in freedom. There is also information about the action we can take to support them.

### Sixth stage – What next for freedom?

Sit and look at the horizon. It is limitless – so are our possibilities when we take on the freedom that God offers us through his Spirit. Where do we go next with him?

As you leave this section there will be a bowl of coloured paper clips Take one as a sign of forging new links – but this time in a chain of freedom with God.

### Leaving!

As you leave, look up at the sign and remember: 'My chains fell off, my heart was free. I rose, went forth and followed . . .'

*Be prepared for all kinds of reactions. It is wise always to have someone on duty to answer questions or to give advice about counselling or guidance, if necessary. There are often tears, sometimes of joy, often of regret, or real grief. Our experience with this particular labyrinth was that at the stage when people looked into the hand mirror and touched their own face, with the knowledge that God loved that face as his own child, they often felt moved for the very first time to know just how much God loved them.*

Labyrinths are not for everyone. Some people will move round very quickly and not see any sense in it. Others may well stay there for hours! But they have proved their effectiveness and can be a life-changing experience.

Try one!

# I WANT TO FIND OUT ABOUT SPIRITUAL THINGS (2)

## Quiet Days

Quiet Days are used for times of reflection and introspection.

They may be held on church premises, but many groups move away from their normal base of worship into a smaller, quieter space – a country church, or a retreat centre or anywhere that peace and quiet can be almost guaranteed.

Most Quiet Days have a theme chosen by the leader for that day, so the material offered here is given simply as a guide for reflection. Almost all of it is the product of such reflective quietness and many people feel moved to put their thoughts into writing. Encourage this. Also encourage the sharing of these pieces, where people are prepared to do so. The shared insights can add to the day for those who cannot put their thoughts into their own words.

First a hymn, set to a folk tune. Perhaps it could be sung by a single voice, with the words available for people to sing to themselves as the day goes on.

**Through this day of quiet and calm**       **Hymn**

Through this day of quiet and calm
let your peace sink into my soul.
In this place, with time out of time,
send your grace that I may be whole.

In my world of day-to-day cares,
stress and strain can trouble my mind.
Here, today, Lord, grant me the space;
calm my fears and help me unwind.

God, who spoke to waken the world,
speak today with challenge and choice.
Touch my life with wisdom and power.
Let me catch the tone of your voice.

LM    Tune: SCARBOROUGH FAIR

Now some reflective pieces – poetry, hymns and prayers – to be used with a group, or as individuals. It may be useful to make a selection of such pieces available for private times of solitary contemplation.

**Take time**

Take this time,
this gift of time,
sink into its depths
of emptiness;
relax into unscheduled space.

Take this time,
time out of time,
to use for your own purpose.
Open again
the door to self,
the individuality of thought
prompted by nothing more
than personal preferences.

Take this time,
space within time,
to stretch
body, mind, imagination,
to re-energize the spirit.

Take this time,
God's time in your time,
to fall in love with life again.

**Each church should be
a stopping place**     **Hymn**

Each* church should be a stopping place
here in the movement of our days;
a space, somewhere to find ourselves,
amid this curling, madding maze.

Caught in this moment let us rest
and find in silence God is good;
that in this whirl, this twist of pain
the love of God is understood.

Within this instant let us stay
the driven urgency and press,
the onward rush, the ceaseless train,
the reason for our fear and stress.

Be still, and know that God is here,
let love enfold and grace becalm;
yes, rest awhile, and rest in God,
and feel the spirit's soothing balm.

LM    Tunes: WILLIAMS or GONFALON ROYAL
*'Each' can be replaced with 'this' in specific situations.

**Silent day**

You have to listen to silence
for silence is not absence of sound,
but made of tiny voices.

Find an empty place
to be silent
and listen.

Listen to air breathing,
trickling of unseen water,
birds calling, singing,
trees moved by the breeze
and, beyond sight,
faint murmurs
of the inescapable technology
of our time.

Find solace in silence,
but recognize
that even your own breathing
disturbs its totality

and life is never entirely empty.

**Quietness**

Solitude,
serenity?
I long for them –
they rarely come.


I find my ears straining
for every movement –
cars passing, birds singing,
the hum of central heating.
The slightest sound,
though sought,
distracts.
My mind clicks with connections,
peace eludes me.


But take me to the seashore
with waves crashing and
        gulls crying;
or to the mountain top
where you can almost hear
        the clouds move;
or to the waterfall, or stream,
rushing, gushing on its way.
There, in nature's sounds,
I find that solitude I seek.
And can be still.

## Quiet Day?

Lord, I'm not good at quiet contemplation.
After some time in silence
my mind shoots off in odd directions –
and there's a draught from somewhere!
Others sit, eyes closed,
expressions rapt and body language stilled,
the very epitome of prayer.
My gaze wanders to woodwork
and windows,
from candles to crosses,
but my mind is not on you.
Or is it?

In the wooden beam next to me
there is a knot
and there's another.
How clever of the hand that shaped the wood
to make a feature of the faults.
Candles and windows
make points of light, defeating darkness.
Crosses, one simple wood,
another in window glass –
is it a lighthouse,
or a cross –
and does it matter?

Now – I must concentrate.
My prayerless mind is wandering from you.
Or is it?

Lord, take my knotted thoughts
and shape them for your purpose.
Let flickering, fractured light
make points of reference for me.
And cross, or lighthouse,
stand as symbol
of direction and assurance.

Lord, you are here,
even in my inattentiveness.

Sometimes, when concentration is hard to achieve, it can be helpful to have objects on which to focus – in this case, a pebble.

Flowers, crosses – particularly holding crosses – banners, images on a screen, candles, photographs and many other objects can work.

Be imaginative.

### Holding the pebble
That pebble was smooth, hard and cold,
    inanimate,
        unyielding,
            shaped by countless years of pounding seas and rocks.
Like millions more, it seemed –
yet not the same.
And as I held it in my hand,
exploring shape
    and size
        and texture,
            it changed –
absorbed my warmth,
darkened with moisture –
took something from me
which made a difference,
even if only for a while.

The world is hard
and shaped
    by circumstance
        and time,
but maybe
for a while,
even there,
I can make a difference.

Contemplating a sanctuary lamp in Christ's and Notre Dame Chapel, Liverpool Hope University:

## Do not resist the symbolism of a burning light

Do not resist the symbolism of a burning light
that indicates belief that God
is here both day and night.

Do not decline the imagery of Christ upon the cross,
reminder of the depth of love
that suffered utter loss.

Do not discard the images, the candles, icons, flowers,
that trigger feelings deep within
through sacramental powers.

Do not despise these things so different from your own,
they speak of God's variety
and show you're not alone.

Quietness and contemplation lead to introspection and often a sense of real and personal closeness to God. And we need to express that in words.

When there is time to think, that is the time when we remember that God seems to have sent certain people to us for the specific purpose of showing us how much we are wrapped in love. It is God's love, but shown in the care and warmth offered by others in those times when we need it most.

## I love my God with all my heart          Hymn

I love my God with all my heart,*
I thank God that I'm living,
enfolded, folded in that love,
and all my life I'm giving.

The deepest love, beyond the love
of our imagination,
outlasts the love that dies at death
and this is God's intention.

I fell into that well of love
while round me hell was ringing;
I sang God's praise and grasped the gift
that grace alone was bringing.

Now God has wrapped me in such love,
beyond my expectation;
and I will live and love again
in praise for re-creation.

8.7.8.7   Tune: HOW CAN I KEEP FROM SINGING
*could be used after a divorce, on a second marriage etc.

## Sometimes a darkened sky

Sometimes a darkened sky
infects my mind
and life is arid
stark, unkind;
and, fathom as I might,
I miss the light
and all seems night.

Then at the crest of my distress
you thunder through the waves
        of fear,
caress with words
of gentleness,
and soothe me back to sense
and faith,
to rippling,
slowly settling,
calm and peace,
without my knowing what you do . . .

Enfolded in your love,
I sink within your care,
safely.
The warmth that is you
folds round me
in my child's frightened darkness.
You take me to the dawn,
to safe awakening,
never to be lost again.

## God breaks upon my shore    Hymn

God breaks upon my shore,
erodes my unbelief;
no cataclysmic thunderous roar,
no sudden sharp relief.

My faith is fuelled by doubt,
integrity commands
a clear agnostic openness,
that's what my faith demands.

I change from day to day
as love informs my sense,
an imperceptible demand
that needs no recompense.

This grace of God is free,
is never won or earned,
we see a change that's wrought by love,
that's how it is discerned.

Yes found, now found, by love!
And my whole being leaps
with joy and praise, with life and hope,
God's solace never sleeps.

SM    Tune: CARLISLE
A description of a gradual return to faith from agnosticism. The last line of the last
verse alludes to Ps. 121.

During quiet times there is often the opportunity for reflection on the
contrast between this time and everyday life. We can have so many
difficulties in dealing with other people.

## Conversation

Listening God, you are concerned with our conversations. You hear our sharp
debates. You are aware of our differences of opinion. You encourage our
attempts at reconciliation. You rejoice when we begin to understand each
other and find those links which draw us closer together.

As Jesus debated with his opponents, repeated his teaching for those who
were slow to understand and listened to endless problems and questions, so
keep our minds open to possibilities we have not yet considered and aware of
the challenges we must face as we move forward.

Teach us to be patient in our listening.

# I WANT TO FIND OUT ABOUT
# SPIRITUAL THINGS (3)

## Something Musical

Worship is often very wordy. Sometimes it is helpful to use something different. Here is another idea that might be used on a Quiet Day, or in an entirely different context.

The idea of a musical liturgy developed as a means of enabling people of many different nationalities to worship together. Words can be used linked with the music (in hymns or songs, for instance) but the unifying thread is that of music. The words must not dominate.

In practice the intention is to produce a liturgy in which all the elements of worship are presented, but in the form of music rather than the spoken word. Musical taste is very subjective and so this runs the risk of, and this is no pun, hitting the wrong note. Care is needed and, when possible, a knowledge of the congregation or group which is going to participate. Having said that, this style of worship has been well received by multi-national groups and small, local mono-cultural congregations alike. The outline that follows is a suggestion.

The concept of using mostly music for the liturgy should be explained. If items are used in which people can join in singing or playing instruments, words and music should be supplied, but all the suggestions here are available as recordings.

The liturgy is split into traditional, though non-eucharistic, sections. The notes in blue indicate the sort of music that is suggested. The following words in black can be used to set the scene of each section if required or they can be written on an order of service.

Items of music in each category are suggestions and may be mixed and matched or replaced with other items. An attempt has been made to use music of different styles and from different national sources. It is hoped that sufficient detail has been given to enable users to track down recordings of the suggested items.

## Call to worship

Music which provides for invocation, which offers praise:

Our time together begins with music to bring us to worship, to remind us of the presence of God –

**Traditional Religious:** Blessèd city, heavenly Salem (Latin – in translation)
**Contemporary Religious:** Enter into Jerusalem, from the CD *Caribbean Praise*
**Classical Religious:** Introitus (from *Missa pro defunctis*) Duarte Lobo (Portuguese)
**Classical:** *Organ Symphony*, 3rd Movement, Saint Saens (French)
**Secular:** Prologue, *Jonathan Livingston Seagull*, Neil Diamond (USA)

*Silence*

## Confession and seeking forgiveness

Quieter items which enables penitence through which we can seek God's and each other's forgiveness:

We consider our place in creation, the good and bad of our lives, and we face up to those things which bring us shame, those people with whom we need to be reconciled and those to whom we should offer forgiveness –

**Traditional Religious:** Let all mortal flesh keep silence (Liturgy of St James, fourth century)
**Contemporary Religious:** Jesus, Lamb of God, St Thomas More Group (USA)
**Classical Religious:** Kyrie, Traditional/Byrd (English 1538–1623)
**Classical:** *Adagio for Strings*, Barber (USA)
**Secular:** Love theme from *Spartacus*, Khatchaturian (USA)

*Silence*

## We offer glory to God

Music of joy, wonder and exultation:

We have made peace with each other and with God and now we offer thanks and praise and through the music receive affirmation –

**Traditional Religious:** A mighty fortress is our God, Martin Luther, (German)
**Contemporary Religious:** Este momento, from the CD *Tenemos Esperanza* (Spanish)
**Classical Religious:** Sanctus – Traditional/Guerrero (Spanish but sung in Latin)
**Classical:** Morning from *Peer Gynt*, Grieg (Norwegian)
**Secular:** What a wonderful world, Douglas/Weiss (USA)

*Silence*

## We hear the Old Testament
Music which reflects on the history of our faith and the place of Judaism within the Abrahamic faiths:

The Old Testament has provided the scripture foundation of Judaism, Christianity and Islam. We reflect on that extent and depth of tradition –

**Traditional Religious:** The Lord's my shepherd, Crimond (Scottish)
**Contemporary Religious:** In the beginning God played with the planets, from the CD *Sound Bytes*, Pratt/Lee (English)
**Classical Religious:** And then shall your light break forth, *Elijah*, Mendelssohn (German)
**Classical:** Sleepers wake, Bach (German)
**Secular:** By the rivers of Babylon, Boney M (German but sung in English)

*Silence*


## Reflecting, we think of this world
Music which takes us into the world:

As part of this diverse tradition we live in God's world, find our way in it and here give expression to our faith. We reflect on the world –

**Traditional Religious:** Let all the world in every corner sing, George Herbert (English)
**Contemporary Religious:** For the beauty of the earth, Rutter (English)
**Classical Religious:** The heavens are telling, *The Creation*, Haydn (Austrian)
**Classical:** The lark ascending, Vaughan Williams (English)
**Secular:** Going home, Mark Knopfler (English)

*Silence*


## We hear the gospel
Music which gives expression to the witness and ministry of Jesus:

Through the music and all that it brings to our minds we reflect on what we know of the story and the stories of Jesus –

**Traditional Religious:** Jesus, the name high over all, Charles Wesley, (English)
**Contemporary Religious:** Sound a mystic bamboo song, Wallace (New Zealand, Taiwan)
**Classical Religious:** Ave Maria, Caccini (Italian)
**Classical:** Moonlight Sonata, Beethoven (German)
**Secular:** You've got a friend, James Taylor (USA)

*Silence*

## We respond making our commitment

Music which elicits commitment:

As we become part of the harmony of this music let us reflect on how we should respond, how we should deepen our commitment to God and to each other –

**Traditional Religious:** God be in my head, Rutter (English)
**Contemporary Religious:** Will you come and follow me, Bell/Maule (Scottish)
**Classical Religious:** Miserere, Allegri (Italian)
**Classical:** Spiegel im Spiegel, Arvo Pärt (Estonian)
**Secular:** Love changes everything, Lloyd Webber (English)

*Silence*

## And we depart

Music which takes us back to the world where we live most of our lives:

And we depart back to our homes, our work, to those with whom we share our lives –

**Traditional Religious:** Forth in thy name, O Lord, I go, Charles Wesley (English)
**Contemporary Religious:** We are marching (Siyahumba), (South Africa)
**Classical Religious:** Lord, now lettest thou thy servant depart in peace, Gretchaninov (Russian)
**Classical:** Widor's Toccata (French)
**Secular:** Homeward Bound, Simon and Garfunkel (USA)

*Silence*

## Offering each other a blessing

Music of blessing:

As we go we wish each other God's blessing –

**Traditional Religious:** Shalom chaverim-Hevenu shalom (Jewish)
**Contemporary Religious:** The peace of the earth, Christine Carson & WGRG (Guatamalan) from *There is one among us*, Wild Goose Publications, 1998
**Classical Religious:** Chanson de nuit, Elgar, (English)
**Classical:** Meditation from *Thais*, Massenet (French)
**Secular:** Sabbath Prayer, *Fiddler on the Roof* Bock/Harnick (USA)

# Passover Agape/Lovefeast

## An order for worship

An Agape or Love Feast is a meal celebrated in some traditions which is similar to Holy Communion, but which has the potential to be more inclusive. Bread and water are used rather than bread and wine. The atmosphere is informal, more like an ordinary meal.

The order of service which follows uses this idea, but is also inspired in part by the Jewish Passover. It is based on a service for ecumenical worship held during Holy Week which, because of its informal nature, attracted some people from the fringe of the church, who came out of curiosity.

This worship could be led by a variety of people or by a single voice.

*The following hymn or 'Alleluia! Sing to Jesus'*

**This is the point of our faith for the future**          **Hymn**

This is the point of our faith for the future,
pooling our knowledge of love and of life,
bringing together the world and its people,
working for freedom, an ending of strife.

This is the God that we share, that we worship,
source of all cultures, the ground of all peace,
God in a unity dwelling within us,
growing between us and bringing release.

This is the way we will walk with each other,
walk hand in hand to the end of the way,
sharing each moment, each hope for the future,
bringing to being this dawning new day.

11.10.11.10
Tunes: EPIPHANY HYMN or IN THE BEGINNING GOD PLAYED WITH THE PLANETS

**Introduction**

This is the season of Passover, Pesach. Today we meet as Christians, but we remember our heritage and shared inheritance with the Jewish people. As we share this Agape, this Love Feast, this communion, it is appropriate that we identify with them and so our words are formed from our own Scriptures, but also as an echo of the liturgy for the Passover. For Jews, memory is all important. In memory they are united with those who suffered and lived, loved and rejoiced before them. We echo this as we 'do this in remembrance' of Jesus. And so we share:

We remember tonight that long ago, on a night like this, the people with whom we share our tradition set out on a journey.

They knew enslavement and oppression, but they remembered a happier past. God called them from slavery and offered them the courage to seek freedom. Boldly they left Egypt, crossed the sea, and headed into a desert. They believed that God would bring them to a far-off Promised Land.

The memory of this journey they recounted and we share. It has been passed down from generation to generation. The story was told to children and to children's children, reiterated and re-enacted from year to year.

We too give thanks for our freedom; we too imagine or remember what it means to be a slave.

And so we pray for all who are still in slavery, still denied their human rights. As we meet at this table, we affirm that there is a place at God's table for all people of all ages and all nations.

Here we share a cup of blessing, which speaks of deliverance; here we eat the bread of life, which speaks of freedom and unity.

May we be united with our neighbours of whatever race or creed.

May all people be free from bondage
and from oppression,
from hunger
and from want,
from hatred
and from fear;
may we all be free to think
and to speak,
to learn
and to love;
may God give us hope
and the reason to rejoice;
soon, in our days.
**Amen.**

This is the story that they recounted:
Ex. 12.21–27

*The following hymn or 'Sanna, sannanina'*

**The sacramental waiting        Hymn**
The sacramental waiting
for love that is to come
is like God's constant heartbeat,
the thrumming of a drum.

The things that really matter,
that keep us safe or sane,
are like God's bread that's broken,
like rainbows after rain.

The hope that holds us captive,
the grace that seals our worth,
are God's firm confirmation
that love is ours on earth.

We watch the sunbeams scatter.
The shadows flicker fast.
Yet God's love is a constant,
we know that love will last.

7.6.7.6   Tune: KNECHT

Those people continued their reflection. Whether or not this is our experience, we continue to identify with the Jews as we pray:

Our ancestors were wandering Arameans;
they went down into Egypt and lived there as aliens,
few in number.
In time they became a great nation.
The Egyptians treated them harshly and afflicted them,
by imposing hard labour on them,
they cried to God and God heard their voice and saw their oppression.
God brought them out of Egypt with a terrifying display of power,
and with signs and wonders.
He brought them to freedom and gave them a land flowing with milk and honey. *(based on Deut. 26.5–9)*

Since then our parents in faith have been wanderers, without a home. Again and again, they have been fugitives and refugees.
Through them we share the pain of the outsider, the hopelessness of the oppressed, the distress of the homeless, the dislocation of the refugee.
They have experienced the fear that we see in those around us who come to our shores for refuge.
They were used and abused.
And now we pray to God to help us to remember our own heritage as we meet our neighbours in the strangers on our streets.
We pray for courage to trade fairly and to work for freedom.
Help us to be trustworthy and just in all our relationships and dealings with every person.

Fire our hearts with your love, that we might always strive for freedom and justice.
We make our prayer for the sake of our neighbours and in memory of all who have suffered. **Amen**.

*The following hymn or 'Be known to us in breaking bread'*

## I vow to love my neighbour, whatever race or creed      Hymn

I vow to love my neighbour, whatever race or creed,
to join her in her suffering, to plead with him in need.
This love will always question, will search out right and wrong,
will give itself for justice, for those who don't belong.
This love will never falter, till every soul is free,
till nations held in bondage can sing of liberty.

Through scenes of devastation, through famine, drought and war,
we'll work in ways of gentleness, work hard till we restore
the vision of the people, the hope of human grace,
till nations dwell in peacefulness together in this place;
till all the world together can sing in joyful praise;
till all have found communion together in our days.

13.13.13.13.13.13   Tune: THAXTED

And we now move to our remembrance:
Mk. 14.12–25

*The following hymn or 'Author of life divine'*

## Bread of life and cup of blessing      Hymn

Bread of life and cup of blessing,
taken in humility,
help us stand in need together,
strengthened by humanity.

Here the bread is taken, broken,
while our broken lives display
need of love from one another,
need of comfort in this day.

As the wine is poured in blessing,
common cup to pass and share;
equally, we offer gladly
patient love, attentive care.

Held by bonds that can't be broken,
strong in solidarity;
bread of life and cup of blessing,
symbolize our unity.

8.7.8.7   Tune: ALL FOR JESUS

## The sharing
*Bread and water are shared, with people serving one another.*

*The following hymn or 'Because thou hast said'*

## The stranger is welcomed, the enemy blessed          Hymn
The stranger is welcomed, the enemy blessed,
a scandalous gospel that Jesus professed;
but can we adopt such a dangerous stance,
forgetful forgiveness, love caught in a glance?

We harbour resentment and hatred is rife;
the past shades the present and fractures each life;
we love to be certain, to cage or constrain,
the people who challenge we view with disdain.

God, let us be Christ to the ones that we meet,
as willing to serve as to sit at your feet.
God, give us the courage to see in each face
the Christ who has shown how to live with your grace.

11.11.11.11   Tune: DATCHET

**May God who has led his people through the ages lead us on the paths of peace out into the world, to serve and to work in his name. Amen.**

*After the blessing an ordinary informal meal may be shared while conversation continues.*

# I WANT TO FIND OUT ABOUT
# SPIRITUAL THINGS (4)

## Pilgrimage

People have made pilgrimages since the day they first discovered that there is some 'other', some 'god', and that there are special places to go to meet with that 'other'. So they climbed to hilltops to watch the sun rise, or took offerings to rivers and streams, or danced round trees, or built stone monuments without leaving any record of their purpose. Today there are pilgrimages to the homes of the famous, or to the mud of a rock music festival, or to a football stadium or cricket ground.

Christian pilgrimages presumably began – although we have no record of this – when the first curious crowd turned up to see the site of one of the miracles of Jesus, or the place where they crucified him, or the empty garden tomb. There are sites all over the world where faithful pilgrims make arduous journeys to visit a famous church, a holy shrine, or the place where Jesus may have walked. Many people who would not claim to be religious are still over-awed, or moved, by the atmosphere of a vast cathedral or a simple church.

One way of connecting with such people is to organize a pilgrimage walk, with an open invitation for anyone to join in. If there is a famous religious site nearby, then the walk could incorporate that. But any local area can be used for a pilgrimage. To walk around the area in which a local run-down church is situated and then to stand outside and to pray for the people who make up that church and the community they serve can be a moving and meaningful experience. Better still is to move inside and to pray with a disheartened congregation. That can be a very powerful time.

If there are people who would feel uncomfortable with such places, then use the local environment to focus on other things. Make your way to a place where there is a viewpoint over the local community and meditate on the people and the lives that are spread before you. Find the local beauty spot that is fast becoming a rubbish-tip and think about that, and do something about it. Go to as quiet a place as you can find and recognize how different that is from our normally busy, noisy lives. Try to plan a route that will include as many different elements as possible. Think of the routine of life – places of work, transport, supermarkets and shops and small businesses. Think of the stages of life – maternity services, education, health, homes and retirement homes. Think of leisure and of spiritual issues and places. Pray about local government and the issues of the day – maybe outside the town hall and the offices of the local newspaper. There are many places worthy of a pilgrimage – some of them precisely because they are the last places you would think of visiting. Yet showing concern and care for the local area is a vital part of our Christian witness. Inviting others to join in a pilgrimage walk to demonstrate this concern may be one way of communicating the astonishing news that God is not just confined to the church, or to church people.

As your pilgrimage will be unique to your situation, the following material should be used in whatever way you feel is appropriate – or use this as a pattern to stimulate your own thought.

Even the act of walking together can help reflection. When you begin there is no knowing how long the journey will take, or what discoveries will be made on the way.

## Travelling

Why is the journey out
so much longer than
the journey back?
Are there more miles?
Or is it simply
a matter of perspective?

Can the way we travel forward,
not knowing what lies ahead,
make the distance
stretch beyond existing length
into an eternity
of longing to be there,
with the journey safely ended?

And, as we turn
from what we have attained
back to the known
and pre-existing,
is it the familiarity
of signposts passed before
that makes the returning
so much swifter?

Or is there something deeper,
more profound;
that travelling once
a new uncharted way
makes viewpoints change,
so that this road,
this journey,
can never be the same again?

The whole of life is a journey and never more exciting than if we follow God's lead.

**Unexpected God**

Unexpected God
when we follow you
we never know what is round the next corner,
but that is all a part of the package we accept
when we take up your call.
You constantly surprise us with new challenges
and sometimes test our faith to the limits,
but you will always make sense of it later
if we keep trusting you.

Keep us on the road,
constantly moving on in our pilgrimage of faith
and ever ready for the next turning point –
whatever it may be.

**Exciting God**

Exciting God, we pray for those people of vision and initiative
who place new challenges before us
and encourage us to catch their vision.
That is not always easy
and we do not necessarily greet these ideas with enthusiasm.

Forgive us our lack of courage.
Fire our imaginations.
Teach us to be more like those first disciples of Jesus
who had no idea what to expect,
yet were prepared to attempt to follow their calling.
Excite us with your vision of your kingdom come on earth –
through the work that we do as Christians.

In the community there are many lonely people, particularly in older streets, or in sheltered housing, or retirement homes. Think about them.

## Silence

The room is still, although the clock ticks on
and noise is filtered by the empty air.
The gate, next door, clicks out a 'welcome home'
and children chatter on their way from school.
The traffic passes in the street outside;
a siren sounds, a police car rushes by.
A child shrieks out in play and calls a friend
and soon a noisy game of football starts.

But in the room these sounds are lost, ignored
by that lone figure spellbound in the chair,
deaf to the living, loving, breathing world;
wrapped in himself and drowned in memories.
Those were the days of laughter and of tears,
when all the house was ringing out with love.
But now, alone, he hears the bitter truth –
the saddest silence is the lonely heart.

Meditation takes many forms, but sometimes it is difficult to hold the thoughts and to remember them.

### Butterfly mind

Elusive thought
flutters around
the edge of memory.
Settles for a while,
to be captured gently,
handled delicately,
before it flies
into oblivion.

The life of a butterfly
is beautiful,
but brief.

Looking down at hospitals and schools, homes and churches, remember the people who inhabit the buildings or use them at crucial points in their lives.

**A child of God**

A child of God
thrust into the world
wrinkled, red-faced and bloodied,
yelling for breath.
Unaware
of the indignity of birth;
needing food, sleep, protection.
Vulnerable,
yet brimming with possibilities.

A child of God,
rebellious youth.
Argumentative, opinionated;
constantly searching;
experimenting dangerously;
unaware
of the consequences.
Hurtling headlong
into the future.

A child of God
searching for love.
Looking for perfection
through complex emotions
of compromise.
Totally aware
of vulnerability;
yet restless in the quest
for fulfilment.

A child of God,
mature adult;
stressed, burdened and troubled
by responsibilities.
Barely aware
of mortality.
Only concerned to appear
successful.
Coping with life.

A child of God
preparing to die.
Wrinkled and pale,
struggling for breath.
Aware
of the indignity
of helplessness.
Waiting for sleep.
Looking to new life.
Completion!

Looking down over the place where you live or work gives an entirely different perspective to what has become a very familiar scene. Rooftops are evocative, as we imagine what lies beneath them.

## Rooftops

Rooftops put lids on living;
enclosing,
shutting off contents
from curiosity.

Could we lift the lid
on mystery boxes;
turn the key,
let out the music,
open interiors to the air . . .

. . . would we find
velvet-lined luxury,
plain-pine poverty,
brash, flash imitation,
or a single shining jewel?

Boxes and lids
stay closed
to us.
God knows how much
there is of worth
within . . .

## Viewpoint

Living at ground level,
we reduce the sky to memory.
Buildings enclose;
pavements beneath
become controllable,
within our scope.

Here,
above our everyday,
space is on a different scale.
Clouds dominate.
Horizons stretch imagination.
Streets dwindle to lines
and distant people
move into insignificance.

From this viewpoint
a new perspective opens.
God paints a wider picture
and asks us to look again.

Natural beauty is all around us, even in cracks in paving stones, or on grass verges or wasteland. We need to take time to stop and reflect.

## Wild flowers

One single flower
can stop you in your tracks,
break through the barriers of
    not seeing
and make you look.

Even a daisy can do it.
Small, delicate,
pink-tinged perfection.
Or a dandelion,
brash and showy,
glaring gloriously from a
    roadside verge.

Take time to look.
Examine all the evidence.
Colour and beauty
holding such sway in the
commonplace?
Surely natural selection
should have ruled that out?
Why go to all that trouble
to design a weed?

Wherever we go we cannot escape traffic . . .

## Streams of traffic

Streams of traffic hum through life,
a disregarded background to
    our days.

Convenient, inconvenient;
help and hazard; pleasure, pain;
essential, yet disruptive;
the traffic flow moves on,
carrying us to known
and unknown destinations.

Watching the constant change
and interchange, the ebb and flow
controlled by lights and signals,
we become aware
that every journey leads
    to somewhere,
has a purpose, or becomes an
    end within itself.
The stream sweeps us to the
    next place –
wherever it may be –
leaving behind
the ripples of our presence
    on the past.

Often unnoticed.

## Outside the Town Hall

This is a seat of power.
In this place are people who have volunteered to be elected to make decisions that affect our daily lives.
In this place there are debates and differences of opinion.
In this place party politics can seem to make a mockery of the democratic process.
In this place there are honest people trying to make a real difference to the place where they live.

In this place there is pomp and ceremony alongside practical work of the most basic kind.
In this place there are people whose jobs make them unpopular and targets for ridicule or abuse.
In this place there are people who put on a harsh face to protect themselves against their own vulnerability.
In this place there is continuous pressure to resolve insoluble problems and to meet constant demands.

Understanding God, you know the problems faced by the people who work for and serve this community. Help us to be more tolerant in our views of officialdom, recognizing the humanity behind the public face of this building.
Bless those who work here, especially those who feel that they are misunderstood, simply because of the nature of their work.
Bless those who are elected to serve this community and give them wisdom in their decision-making.
Teach us to be more supportive and to play our part in serving where we live.

**Outside the closed door of a church**

This building has been set aside
for God,
for prayer
and for people.

It is a symbol in its place,
though often disregarded
by those who hurry by
on their way to living.
Some will not even know
why it is here,
or what possible use it could be
to this community.
Its doors are shut,
maybe for security,
but the world is kept outside.

God of this community,
bless the people who attend this church.
Support and encourage them
when their work seems to have no effect.
Fire their hearts with love
for the community in which they are set.

Lift their spirits
when they find it difficult to carry on.
Strengthen their faith.
Grant them continuing hope.
Confirm them in your love.
Hold them in your care.

We are all a part of the Body of Christ.
Show us how to offer
willing and working hands
wherever and whenever
they are needed.


Inevitably there will be a place where litter has been left.
It would be sensible to take plastic sacks and gloves to deal with this and to
make the effort a part of the prayer.


## Rubbish

Dear God, look at what some people do to make a mess of this place.
We feel such a sense of despair at the evidence of thoughtlessness, or
laziness, or deliberate destruction that we see around us.
Do people not care?
Do they have no sense of responsibility at all?
Is this just a symptom of a society that doesn't care what kind of a mess it
makes, but does expect someone else to clear it all up?

As we pick up these pieces, help us to reflect on the way our throwaway
society encourages such behaviour.

Are we completely free of its influence in our own lives?

Can we condemn others and entirely condone our own behaviour?

Dear God,
we know that we are not always as careful of your creation as we ought to be.
We bear the responsibility of using the resources you offer us wisely and with
due economy, only taking our fair share.
We confess that there are times when we are careless in our behaviour and
selfish in our attitudes.
We are aware that there are times when we take things – and people – for
granted and treat them thoughtlessly.
We recognize that there are times when we make a mess of things and then
expect someone else to clear it all up.
God, forgive us, and teach us to be more responsible.

# THE BIBLE MAKES NO SENSE TO ME

For many people the Bible is an ancient book with no relevance for them. They may be put off by the language and the apparently fairy-tale nature of some of the stories. For some it may rank with the Harry Potter books or *The Lord of the Rings*.

How can we make this book live? A bit of lateral thinking perhaps? The art of storytelling? After all, human nature hasn't changed that much and the questions we ask are 'as old as the hills'. . . literally.

**God said . . .**

Look at it this way,
said God,
whether I created the universe in six days,
or six billion years,
there was no one else around to see,
so there are none of those historical records
that people seem to need
to give clear evidence
of how it all happened.

Geologists read history
in rocks and valleys.
Archaeologists dig up ancient sites
and compete
to find the earliest signs of human habitation.
Astronomers look to the stars.
Scientists formulate theories.

But the debates go on.
When? Why? How?
And even who originated life?

Because no person was there
when it all began,
there are endless stories and ideas
and people will argue about it for ever.
Look at it this way,
said God,
there are some parts of life
that will always remain a mystery,
but I did my best
to make certain things very clear indeed . . .

## God, help us make sense of your wonder and word        Hymn

God, help us make sense of your wonder and word,
interpreting, sharpening what might be blurred,
enlighten our study, breathe life and bring light,
bring humour and parable, gentleness, might.

The hist'ry, tradition, the reason, the ways
of people of faith give a ground for our praise.
The story of Jesus can counter our fears:
a window on God, through our laughter and tears.

Your spirit is living, but let it be real,
aligned to our intellect, something we feel;
a manifestation of Christ and the cross,
a challenge we hear for our gain or our loss.

Your word is for here, yet for all of the earth,
your word is defining our life and new birth,
your word is transforming our thoughts and our lives,
the gift and the goal to which all of faith strives.

11.11.11.11    Tune: AWAY IN A MANGER


When people have difficulty with the Bible, humour can be used as a way towards opening up a story. Young and old can be made to feel at ease. It can also act as a means of sharing what can otherwise seem irrelevant or churchy . . .


## The serpent's tale

I'm the snake from the Garden of Eden –
a slithery giant-sized worm.
My voice is a menacing sibilant sound –
designed to make everyone squirm.

You may think you know all my adventures –
they're there in the Bible, you see.
But try looking at it from my point of view.
Just think what it's like to be me!

Everybody casts me as the villain –
the very first snake in the grass.
But what makes you think that it's always my fault?
I think you should blame that young lass!

It was great in the Garden of Eden
with only the animals there.
We all had a place, we could find our own space,
lots of food and with plenty to spare.

There were four great big rivers flowed from it
and masses of all kinds of trees.
The dogs were in heaven, they ran round all day,
which was very good news for the fleas.

Then along came this creature called Adam.
Then God said he called him a man.
He'd only two legs and walked upright and straight,
which, to me, didn't seem a good plan.

With the man in the Garden of Eden
the atmosphere started to change.
He set out to give all the animals names,
so it all got to be a bit strange.

Now I ask you, why go to the trouble
of calling that longneck 'giraffe'?
He re-named an ape to an orang-utan!
It's enough to make anyone laugh.

He got carried away by the horses –
called some asses and donkeys and such.
And the beautiful black-and-white striped one he named
a zebra – now that's a bit much!

By the time he had done all his naming,
he wasn't a popular bloke.
The toad thought his name was as ugly as sin
and the earwig was ready to choke.

The anteater foresaw a big problem –
a diet restriction in sight.
Hyenas were laughing, they thought it a joke,
but the pig thought his name wasn't right.

So throughout the great Garden of Eden
some discontent started to stir.
Then, though it was quite bad enough with the man,
God made more of a problem with her!

You see, Adam had felt a bit weary
and God knew he needed some aid,
so while the man slept, he took out a spare rib
and from that bit the woman was made.

At first sight she was very appealing
and Adam was quite overcome.
To judge by the way he reacted to her
she would very soon be a new mum.

They were given the Garden of Eden
to use as a home for their life.
With food and provisions, what more could be done,
for this very first husband and wife?

They could eat from each tree in the garden –
God put a ban only on one –
and that's where the humans show weakness of will
and where we thought that we could have fun.

For, in spite of the tale in the Bible,
that puts all the blame upon me,
those poor misnamed animals wanted them out
because then they thought they would be free.

So they urged me to get at the woman
and cast in her mind some great doubt,
'Did God really say not to eat of that fruit?'
and 'He wouldn't just throw you both out.'

It must be my sibilant syllables,
or maybe the charm in my eyes,
but Eve just fell for it and gave some to him
and then that really opened their eyes!

There was such a mad dash for the fig leaves,
I nearly got squashed on the way.
They hid out of sight in the bushes till night
in the hope God would not come that day.

But they couldn't fool God with their dressing
and, when he knew what they had done,
he banished the pair from the garden for life
to a life of hard toil in the sun.

Before leaving the Garden of Eden
the pair put the blame upon me,
'cos he accused her and then she accused me
and God didn't seem to disagree.

I would like to have blamed all the others,
but God didn't give me a chance.
'You'll crawl on your belly the rest of your days.'
So what chance do I have for romance?

I'm the snake from the Garden of Eden,
though I'm not to blame, you can see,
for thousands of years I've been given a bad name,
but I've told you, it wasn't just me!

And another *tail*, or should that be *tale* . . .

## Mrs Noah

Thank goodness for that!
Fresh air at last! I can't believe it!
And you can't imagine what it's like in there.
The smell! The noise! The overcrowding!

Well, what did he expect it would be like when he crowded all those people and animals together? It may look like a big boat from the outside, but there were far too many creatures in there for any of us to have any comfort.

And can you imagine how difficult the whole performance was from the start?

What would you say if your husband came in one day and told you he was going to build a gigantic boat and make sure that all the family was safe inside it when the floods came?

When the floods came?
What on earth was he talking about?
We were living in one of the driest places on earth: sun beating down every day: no rain for – oh, I don't know how long. And he was setting up a boatyard!

I'd always suspected there was something not quite right about him. His whole family were a bit 'out of touch', should we say? But I'd been betrothed to him since I was a child and didn't have any say in the matter of marriage, so what could I do?

And he'd been a good husband. Given me three strong sons and always tried to keep the family decent and God-fearing, even when the rest of the world didn't seem to care.

But I definitely thought the God-fearing bit had gone too far when he came home with this scheme for the boat. He believed it was God's will!

I humoured him.
After all, he'd started great schemes before and then abandoned them after a while. This one would probably go the same way.

It was when the boat started to tower over the town that I began to wonder about his sanity. And then he insisted that I had to make sure that our sons and their wives were ready to come with us into this 'ark', as he called it.

Well, it took some time to persuade the boys to come – and even longer to convince their wives. They're good girls, but you could understand that they were concerned about being cooped up in that strange place, far away from their friends and families. None of the children could see much sense in it and all I could do was to ask them to put up with it for a few days, just to humour him, and then they could all leave.

At that point, Noah nearly sent us all mad!
He told us about the animals.

Yes! Animals! And birds – and creepy-crawlies and insects as well.
Two of everything – for breeding purposes, of course. And seven of the creatures that God considered 'clean'.

'How are we going to do that?' I yelled.
'And where will we put them all? And how will we feed them? And how can you collect them in the first place?'

'Oh, God will see to all that,' he said – with complete sincerity.

'Huh!' was all I could manage.

So, I had to go back to the boys again and plead for them to come – if for nothing else, at least they could help to look after the animals.
Only later, when I'd finally persuaded them I really needed their help, did I remember how many childhood promises had been broken.

'It's all right, mother,' they'd said, 'we'll take care of . . .' whatever it was at the time. But who had ended up doing all the dirty work?
Well, who do you think?

So my supply list for the ark had plenty of cleaning equipment on it.

You know what happened, of course?
The rains came. The floods came.
We were all crammed into the boat with the animals and we've been sailing for months.

It's just as well that the rabbits breed like . . . rabbits – and that most of the other small creatures, and the insects, do the same. We'd have had great difficulty feeding the larger animals, and ourselves, otherwise.

But, by the end of this adventure, all the animals were feeling the pinch.
I didn't know that a tiger could look at a rhinoceros with such a ferociously hungry stare.

And the cleaning problems!

It's just as well that there were three levels in the boat. The bottom one is extremely full of some very disgusting material. Even the dirtiest animals had moved up to the second level by the end of the voyage.

All Noah could say was that at least it was good ballast and it would make sure that we never capsized.

But, at last, we're on dry land.

It's the top of a mountain, of course, and a long way to go down!
But the boat's stopped rocking and the animals are out sniffing the air and gradually leaving, so perhaps we can get back to some kind of normal life.

It's so quiet round here. No other people.

But Noah says that's good.
God wanted us to start afresh in a new place and to make a new family tribe
– one that believes in God.

At least part of that should keep the boys and their wives busy and happy!

And today we saw these wonderful colours in the sky, shaped like a bow over
the earth.
Noah said that was a sign from God, too. One promising that the flood was
over and our new life could begin.

But . . .

What about emptying the boat?

What about all that stuff in the bottom of it?

Is that a sign of promise?

I suppose it is.

It'll certainly help us to grow some wonderful new vegetables!


## What do we learn from the Psalms?

Scripture passages sometimes contradict one another. The next item offers a
way of admitting that such contradictions exist and of confronting this issue.

It is assumed that this dialogue will take place in an ordinary act of worship.
The two readers stand at different places, for example, at a lectern and in the
pulpit. Their presence should suggest that either is about to read a Bible
lesson for the act of worship.

*Reader 1 in the pulpit. Reader 2 at the lectern. Both are ready to read. They look at
each other – puzzled. They each start to read simultaneously.*

Reader 1:  Psalm 22.

Reader 2:  Psalm 121.

Reader 1:  Excuse me! I thought you asked me to read Psalm 22?

Reader 2:  I did. But I thought you weren't going to start, so I thought I should.

Reader 1:  But you're not reading the same psalm.

Reader 2:  No. I'm reading Psalm 121.

Reader 1:  So you don't want me to read Psalm 22?

Reader 2:  Yes I do. And I also want to read number 121.

Reader 1:  Two Psalms? Are you sure?

Reader 2: Absolutely!

Reader 1: Sounds strange to me. Anyway, who goes first? I suppose it should be you, seeing as you're the visitor.

Reader 2: Oh no! Surely it should be ladies first?

Reader 1: Maybe! But in the opinion of some of those people out there, I'm no lady!

Reader 2: And we're wasting time! How are we going to resolve this?

Reader 1: I know! Let's be different. Let's read alternate verses. You start!

Reader 2: Psalm 121.

Reader 1: Psalm 22.

Reader 2: 'I lift up my eyes to the hills – where has my help come from?'

Reader 1: 'My God, my God, why have you forsaken me? Why are you so far from saving me, from the words of my groaning?'

Reader 2: 'My help comes from the Lord, the maker of heaven and earth.'

Reader 1: 'O my God, I cry out by day, but you do not answer, by night and am not silent.'

Reader 2: 'He will not let your foot slip – he who watches over you will not slumber.'

Reader 1: Excuse me a minute!

Reader 2: Yes! What now?

Reader 1: Are we reading from the same book?

Reader 2: I hope so! Mine's a Bible and you're reading from the church Bible.

Reader 1: Well, I think there's some kind of discrepancy.

Reader 2: Do you indeed? What is it now?

Reader 1: Well, whoever wrote my psalm couldn't seem to find God anywhere. Your man knows exactly where to find him.
So my man goes round shouting, 'Where are you, God? I want to talk to you!' while yours just ambles off to the hillside to find him.

Reader 2: Yes! Well, they were probably two very different people.

Reader 1: But which of them do I believe?
All these contradictions! I give up! I'm going – and I'll just let you get on with trying to explain that one!

Reader 2: Me! Why me?

*At this point the preacher will explain . . . perhaps!*

Reading through the Bible, we find contrasting and sometimes contradictory themes. We need them all to make sense of the world, our neighbours and of God.

## Dynamic God, the essence of our being      Hymn

Dynamic God, the essence of our being,
foundation of the 'is' and 'is to be',
the origin of all that has been given,
our means of living. Teach us to be free.

Prophetic God, disturb us in our comfort,
then challenge our indifference, face to face.
Bring home the fact that mercy without justice,
or justice without mercy, cripples grace.

Dynamic voice, ring out through all creation,
then speak to every person with your care,
that held within a cosmic contradiction
of judgement, heaven, hell, your love is there.

11.10.11.10   Tune: O PERFECT LOVE

In the Bible, there are stories about Jesus which have been treasured through the years because the human nature they depict is still our nature. Within these stories we can imagine characters that look from a new perspective. Imaginative backgrounds can breathe new life into the stories. Read this before you go to Mk. 2.1–12.

## A person of property

Look what they've done to my roof!
Can you believe it?
A great big gaping hole, open to the sky and to any bird or wildlife that might feel like a visit!
I ask you – who would want to live in a house like this? If I'd wanted to live in the open air, it would have been much cheaper to pitch a tent.
My father built this house while we were still youngsters. I remember being kept well away from the place, in case I got into trouble, or was a nuisance to the men. And now look at it!
There's dirt and grass and mud all over the floor and this enormous hole in the roof. I asked the men who'd done it if they were coming back to repair it, but they were far too excited about their friend to give any sort of sensible answer.

Of course, you'll have heard about what happened to their friend, I suppose?
I know I'd never have invited Jesus in if I'd known all the bother it would cause. I just thought I'd really make a bit of a name for myself by being able to persuade Jesus to come to my house.

Everyone was talking about him – about his stories, about the miracles – and apparently his teaching was down-to-earth and well worth listening to. He was quite a celebrity. So it was a feather in my cap when he accepted my invitation.

But it didn't take me long to recognize that I may have made a very big mistake. I was very happy to welcome Jesus and some of his prominent followers into my home, but I soon found out that I wasn't going to be able to shut the door behind them and a whole crowd of folk were all pushing to get inside. It was impossible to fit everybody in and soon the street was crowded and there were people climbing up trees and on to rooftops and peering into the windows. It was like being under siege. I knew there was someone on the outside stairs, but I couldn't get out to do anything about it.

The first sign that there was anyone on the roof was when bits of dirt started dropping from the ceiling – although most people took no notice, they were too absorbed in what Jesus was saying.
I couldn't concentrate on him. I was too concerned with the welfare of my property, especially when the noise on the roof got louder and I suddenly started to see daylight through the holes!
Next minute, the daylight had gone and there was a face peering down at me. Then the hands started to make the hole bigger. Not just one pair of hands, mark you! Soon there were eight hands scrabbling at the ceiling and the hole was becoming more noticeable to everybody in the room.

Finally, Jesus looked up, and just at that point all the hands and the peering heads moved away and I was furious. They'd made a hole in my roof and they weren't even using it for anything!
But the daylight disappeared again and the hole was filled with what looked like a big bundle of clothes. What on earth was happening? Was this an invasion? Somebody trying to harm Jesus? I was really concerned and quite relieved to find that the bundle was actually a man on some kind of matting and that they were lowering him down towards Jesus. When they managed to clear just enough space on the floor to let the bundle down, it was clear to see that the man was in a dreadful state. He couldn't move at all, apart from his head and a faint movement in his hands, but he looked at Jesus with such a mixture of despair and hope that even I felt sorry for him.

You could see that Jesus really felt for the man, but that he was also looking up at the roof where four faces were anxiously looking in to see if Jesus could help. And it was as he looked at the faces that he began to smile. If they'd been prepared to go to all that trouble to bring their friend to him, you could see Jesus was trying to tell them it was going to be all right.

And that's when the miracle happened. One minute the man was lying there helpless, the next he was getting up – hesitantly at first, but certainly up on his feet – and the place was in an uproar.

Apparently the paralysed man was well known to many of the crowd and they were shouting and congratulating him and rushing around talking about what had happened. The healed man was just anxious to get back to his friends and they were trying to push their way back down the stairs to greet him. Some of the lawyer types left in disgust because Jesus had healed the man by forgiving him his sins, which they thought was blasphemous. So Jesus and his followers recognized that it was time to move on.

In no time at all the room was empty – except for me – and all I had was a big mess on the floor and an even bigger hole in my roof!

Who's going to help me to put it all right again, that's what I want to know?

Miracles are all right, in their place – but property is property, after all!

And sometimes it's good to sing these stories. The following song works well with all ages. It is fun if half the congregation sing the verses and the other half responds with the chorus. All join together for the last chorus.

**When Peter stepped out on the water**  **Hymn**

When Peter stepped out on the water,
when Peter stepped out on the sea,
his friends thought his action was silly
and called out to him with this plea –

> *'Come back. Come back. Come back to safety with us, please do.*
> *Come back. Come back. O come back to safety, please do.'*

When Peter stepped out on the water,
when Peter stepped out on the sea,
so sure he could walk out to Jesus –
'It's OK. I'll do it. You'll see.'

> *Chorus*

When Peter stepped out on the water,
the waves underfoot made him think.
He felt the wind roaring around him
and slowly he started to sink.

> *Chorus*

When Jesus saw Peter was sinking,
he said to him, 'Peter, don't fret.
Take hold of my hand and I'll save you.
You've lots more to do for me yet.'

> *'Come here. Step out. Come face adventure with me,' he said.*
> *'Come here. Step out. O come face adventure with me.'*

Irregular    Tune – MY BONNIE LIES OVER THE OCEAN

Jesus told stories all the time and the stories he told were about the everyday things around him. We need to begin to retell our own stories, rooting them in the things that surround us, to communicate the same values and ideas. I live in Scarborough, so let's tell –

## A parable of Scarborough

Three families came to spend a day in Scarborough.

The first family parked their car in a disabled parking space, even though they weren't entitled to – but it was the nearest space to the beach. They couldn't be bothered to walk to the beach, and didn't want to pay for deck-chairs, so they claimed a bench on the promenade and stayed there all day. They grumbled because people kept walking past them and they couldn't see the kids on the sands. The children dropped down onto the nearest bit of sand and that was so soft that they couldn't build sandcastles, and when they dug holes the sand just slid back down the sides and filled the holes in again. It was a long way to the sea and their parents didn't want to walk that far, so the children didn't go there either. Instead they shouted and fought with each other and made a general nuisance of themselves. Their parents shouted at them and argued with each other, until it was time to go to the pub, where the kids spent a lot of time outside feeling bored and wanting to go home.

The second family parked their car in a side street a long way away, to save on parking fees. They carried their chairs and wind-breaks and picnic paraphernalia down onto the firmer sand and set it all up with their backs to the sea, which caused a bit of chaos when the tide crept in behind them. The children built sandcastles, but they were in the path of the donkeys and the sandcastles were trampled down. They went into the sea, but they thought it was far too cold, so they came back to their deck-chairs and the children spent the time sending text messages to their friends on their mobile phones, while their parents went to sleep in the sun and suffered the consequences afterwards. When the tide caught them out, they had to scramble everything to safety and had a long walk back to the car feeling decidedly damp.

The third family walked to the beach. They spent time exploring the rock pools, looking for starfish and shells and crabs. They found a stretch of clear damp sand and built a magnificent castle with turrets and flags and a moat. They splashed in the waves, which weren't cold once you got used to them. They raced along the beach, stopping to pick up shells and to skim pebbles across the waves. They watched the tide swirl around their castle and rescued the flags just before they floated away. They ate their picnic, enjoyed ice-creams, lay in the sun for a while, then faced the walk back, tired, but chattering excitedly about the things they had done together and their plans for tomorrow.

Which one of those families had the best day?

# Phone Talk

From time to time, inside the church, we need to be reminded how far removed we seem to be from those who rarely visit us.

These six pieces were written for a specific service about outreach, to illustrate how many people comce through the church doors very hesitantly, but with a certain amount of interest or need. There are endless possibilities for expansion of this idea – please feel free to adapt these or to write your own.

**Young mum**

'Oh yes, the christening! Yes, it was a lovely day – and with all the family there as well . . . it was just as well that my mother had done the meal. I could never have coped.

Yes, the service was nice. There was another being done at the same time, so the church was packed out. We'd had to see the minister beforehand, of course, and he made it sound a bit more solemn than we thought it was, but I suppose that's fair enough. He has a living to make and it's important to him. And I must admit he did make us wonder whether there was more to this than meets the eye. I mean, I've never thought of myself as being important to God before, but that's how he made it sound.

Anyway, it's something we might think about later. Did you realize that in the service there's one point when the church people promise to look after the faith of the children? Probably that means they'll be getting in touch with us later. I don't mind really – they seemed like nice people. I saw one or two in church who live near us – I suppose they must always go there, 'cos they weren't with us. In fact I passed one lady in the street today. She smiled, but she didn't speak. I suppose she'll be very busy. But I would have liked to ask her what they do about babies if you want to go to church. It seemed friendly, but they might not want little ones crying all over the place. And it would be nice to get to know a few people – we've only been here a year and I get stuck in the house with the baby a lot just now. I don't think I'd go to church on my own though. I'd want to be sure I knew somebody first.

Anyway, I must go – the baby's crying!

See you!'

## The best man

'Oh, hi! Hey, the wedding was great on Saturday. You should have seen us after the reception – three o'clock in the morning we got home and I didn't know where I was! I felt a bit rough on Sunday, I can tell you!

Yes, the weather stayed fine. I got a bit of a surprise at the church though. I mean, it looks real old-fashioned from the outside and I was sure it would be cold and dark, but it was totally different. I mean, they had carpets and chairs with padded seats and it was sort of colourful like – and it didn't really feel like a church 'cos it was warm and it felt quite friendly really.

Hey, the vicar, or the minister, or whatever you call him, was funny though! He had a long black frock on and a sort of decorated thing over his shoulders. He wasn't a bad bloke though – and he didn't seem too bothered when I couldn't find the ring. I could see Pete and Jane were a bit embarrassed, but the vicar wasn't – he just told me to look in my pocket again and – guess where I found it? Stuck in the lining!

Pete and me got there ever so early 'cos Pete was nervous and the vicar came and sat with us for a bit. We were the only ones there! He was telling us that they had a badminton club at the church – he had to advertise, I suppose. But I wouldn't mind going to see what it's like. They might not mind that I'm not really good at it. It didn't seem too bad a place really.

I'll have to find somebody else who knows about it. I wouldn't like to just turn up – they might be a bit exclusive.

I wonder who would know?

Anyway, must go!

See you!'

## The bride

'Oh, hello! It's nice to hear from you!

Yes, we just got back from honeymoon on Sunday. Oh, it was fabulous – the weather was great and that hotel was out of this world – I'm so glad you told us about it. Oh, and thanks for the towels, by the way. They'll be really useful.

The wedding was lovely, wasn't it? I was ever so nervous, you know, but the minister was very nice and I'm sure he was trying to make us feel relaxed. I could have murdered Nick when he couldn't find the ring though! I was so embarrassed! But wasn't the church nice? I'd been into it once before for Julie's baby's christening and I thought then that it would be lovely for the wedding. It's nice and bright and sort of up-to-date, but it still feels as if it's got a bit of history behind it, if you know what I mean. And it's near where we're living as well. We might try to find out what's going on there – it's just round the corner and it might give us a chance to make a few new friends. It'd be one way of feeling like a part of the community. I'd like to feel as if we belonged – 'cos it's not a bad place to live.

I don't know how you go about finding out about things though. I suppose we could ring the minister again, but he's probably forgotten who we are by now – he must meet so many people. Maybe someone who lives round here could tell me. I mean, I can't just walk into the place and say, "Right, what's going on here then?" can I? Well, *I* can't, anyway. And Pete wouldn't come with me – he says they might be all toffee-nosed and holy in there.

Oh, sorry! Must go – the doorbell's ringing.

See you soon. Come for a meal sometime.

Bye!'

## After the funeral
'Hello!

Oh, hello there!

Oh, I'm not too bad you know. I'm managing. You've got to, haven't you? Well, the family's been very good and the neighbour on one side keeps popping in, so people are looking after me at present. It won't go on forever, of course. Folk have their own lives to lead. But maybe I'll be feeling a bit better myself by the time that happens.

Oh, I do miss her though. I didn't realize how much I would, you know! We'd been married for 41 years. It would have been her birthday next week. Oh, I'm sorry, but I still get a bit choked up sometimes. I have a little weep now and then, when I'm on my own – I can't help it. I can't let on to anyone else, of course. I can only tell you because I've known you so long.

The padre chap was good with the funeral and he came to see me before and afterwards – three times! But he'll not be able to do it much longer, I reckon – he said he'd had three funerals the same week and he's got another one in the church tomorrow. He can't keep visiting everyone, can he?

No, I did wonder about going back to the church, but I don't think so. It seemed like a peaceful place and there must be some nice people there, but I don't know any of them and just at present I can't find it in me to go out among strangers. There is a couple down the road that go, but I don't really know them. They always go past in such a hurry on Sunday morning. No, I don't think I will go. Not on my own.

Maybe if you come sometime, you would go with me?

Thanks very much for ringing.

Please keep in touch. It's good to hear a friendly voice.

Goodbye!'

## The Christmas story

'Hi! Hey, did you have a good Christmas?

Yeah! Great, wasn't it? But the money we've spent! And you wonder where it's all got to, don't you? Hey, you'll never guess what! We went to church at Christmas! Yes – really! Do you know, I've never been in my life before – no, we were married in the registry office, remember?

Yes, I probably was christened in church, but I won't remember that, will I?

Well, it was all right. We went 'cos our Darren's in the Boys' Brigade – no, he likes it – we were quite surprised really. Yes, well the B.B. – that's what they call it – they'd been asked to sing a carol and to be in a play about Christmas. Yes, baby Jesus and all that! Our Darren was a shepherd and you should have seen him with a tea-towel on his head and our Debbie's toy lamb under his arm. We had to try not to laugh when he was all dressed up, because he said he wouldn't do it if we laughed. Anyway, it all went all right in the end. We took the camera and sat up in the balcony and we got some great photos – you'll have to see them.

Yeah, it wasn't bad really. We knew some of the carols from the telly and there were some new ones that we didn't know, but they were really good. It was a sort of mixture of old and new. I was amazed there was anything new at all – I thought churches were all old-fashioned.

No, they weren't all old wrinklies! Quite a few were families – sort of all ages, really. Yes, I was surprised. I thought it was all old people as well.

No, I don't think I'll be going again for a while – not unless they have something involving the B.B. I suppose we'll have to go then, for Darren's sake. But I couldn't just walk in any other time, not on my own. I don't think they expect us to go anyway – we don't belong there, after all.

Must go! I can see Debbie coming up the road and her tea's not ready.

See you! Bye!'

**B.B. boy**

'Hi Ben! It's Darren!

What time is your Dad picking us up from the football? Six-thirty? O.K. And what time did they say we'd be home? Mum's going on about it – you know!

Hey, you haven't told anybody about that play at Christmas, have you? I heard Mum talking to someone on the phone about it – and I'd told her not to say anything!

Well, do you want anybody to find out you went to church?

No, B.B.'s all right. It's uniforms and games and things and we work for badges . . . all kinds of things . . . and you have to do drill and learn how to march and we're going on a proper parade soon – and camping in the summer!

Yes, we are supposed to go to Church Parade, but it's not so bad 'cos we all sit together so we can fool about a bit when nobody's looking.

Well, I don't really understand the rest of what goes on in church. We learn a bit in the B.B., but my Mum says I shouldn't take any notice of the religious things – she doesn't want me getting involved in anything like that. She says she's managed without it all her life, so it can't be that important.

Do you think there really is a God?

I bet nobody in church would dare answer that question!

Right, see you later! Half-past six!'

And the stories could go on . . .

# HIGH DAYS AND HOLIDAYS!

There are times when the church is busy beyond the normal. It's difficult for someone on the outside to understand what the fuss is all about. The difficulty is knowing how to welcome visitors who come on those occasions. We have probably all heard comments like, 'Don't see you here often' or 'They only come at Christmas, or harvest, or whatever the occasion might be.' How would we feel coming to church on a special occasion and being talked about like this?

What can we do to make these occasions friendly and accessible? How do we make sure that the language is relevant and that the services and stories are meaningful? What can we say that links the way we worship with the way that these occasional visitors live? Here are some seasonal suggestions:

## Advent

### Advent prayer

There is excitement in the air.
This is the season of anticipation.
For many, it is in the fairytale magic of Father Christmas.
For us, it is because we are waiting to celebrate a birth.

God of hope,
we come to you in the season of Advent
to give you thanks for the hope you offer us.
This world can be a frightening and dangerous place.
All around us there are signs of wars and power struggles and troubles of every kind.
People have turned away from you and are living selfish and ungodly lives.
It seems as if the church has lost its way, too, and its voice is ignored.
In fact, the world today is very much the same as it was 2,000 years ago.

God of hope,
into that situation you sent, first a prophet, then your Son.
At this time of year, we anticipate the birth of your Son, but celebrate the life of the prophet.
As John the Baptist was sent to prepare the way for Jesus, let us now prepare ourselves, by remembering John's fiery words and ringing challenge.
For he is your messenger and we need to be reminded to prepare ourselves again for a new birth.

Advent God, in our worship together, challenge us and renew us and help us to prepare for Christmas in the right way.
For the sake of your Son. Amen.

**In the night      Hymn**

In the night,
women wait.
Bridegroom comes
to the gate.
Lamps are lit,
some too late
for the time of greeting,
so they miss the meeting.

> *We will watch and pray*
> *for his coming day*
> *and we trust,*
> *as he comes,*
> *he will find us waiting.*

In a cold
stable stall
lay a child
for us all,
but so few
came to call
on the baby stranger
lying in that manger.

> *Chorus*

On a cross
on the hill
Jesus died,
stranger still.
Priests were out
for the kill,
and that power would show him
that they did not know him.

> *Chorus*

In our time,
will he come?
Will our lives
find the room
for the one
in whose home
we receive a greeting,
love and judgement meeting?

> *Chorus*

6 6 6.6 6. and refrain    Tune –
THEODORIC

## Advent candle-lighting readings

### First Sunday in Advent – Hope

Reader 1:   Where is Jesus?

Reader 2:   Look! Is that the Christ? He struggles upward with a heavy load. His hope was dashed so long ago. It was dark there, and so long ago. His hope was dashed.

Reader 1:   But he has seen a light and, struggling, he works his way, upward, toward the light. Is that the Christ?

Reader 2:   I see hope in his eyes . . .

*Light candle*

Prayer:   Help us, O God, to move toward your light however great our burden, however steep the slope. Draw us toward your light, and give us hope. Amen.

### Second Sunday in Advent – The Word of God

Reader 1:   I've been reading. But the words are so difficult. I don't always understand.

Reader 2:   The words speak of hope.

Reader 1:   But also of struggle.
Reader 2:   The words speak of light.
Reader 1:   But also of love.
Reader 2:   The words offer life.
Reader 1:   Then the words must be clear to me. Help me to understand.

*Light candles*

Prayer:     Speak your words to us, O God. Words of hope, of light, of love. Words that offer life. And make them plain. Amen.

## Third Sunday in Advent – John the Baptist

Reader 1:   Strange person. All ragged and dirty. Wild in the wilderness. Lost for a penny.
Reader 2:   Who'd listen to him?
Reader 1:   Crowds came.
Reader 2:   Why?
Reader 1:   A strange allure. Spoke in riddles. Offered judgement as a promise.
Reader 2:   Not inviting.
Reader 1:   No invitation necessary. Come freely, he said. Hear truth. See yourselves in the reflection. Understand your need. Repent.
Reader 2:   And what?
Reader 1:   God forgives, that's all.
Reader 2:   It is enough.

*Light candles*

Prayer:     Show us ourselves, Lord.
            Bring us to our knees.
            Forgive and lift us up, Lord.
            Lord, have mercy.
            Christ, have mercy.
            Lord, have mercy. Amen.

## Fourth Sunday in Advent – Mary

Reader 1:   Just a child.
Reader 2:   Waiting.
Reader 1:   Humble and waiting.
Reader 2:   God's servant.
Reader 1:   But just a child.
Reader 2:   What's the point of it all? What was her purpose?
Reader 1:   To give birth to a God. That's all.
Reader 2:   Enough, enough.

*Light candles*

Prayer:     God, give us the humility to hear your call,
            and to do your will,
            whether the task be great or small. Amen.

**Christmas Day**

Reader 1:   All the light of the universe has burst upon the world.
Reader 2:   Blinding.
Reader 1:   A supernova outshone.
Reader 2:   Incredible.
Reader 1:   Christ is born.
Reader 2:   A baby?
Reader 1:   Yes.
Reader 2:   It is enough.
Reader 1:   Indeed! It is! Enough!
Together:   Alleluia! Amen!
**All:**   **Alleluia! Amen!** *(these words may be sung to a suitable setting)*

*Light candles*

Prayer:   All praise to God for light,
for hope, for love, for joy, for faith, for Christmas.

**All:**   **Alleluia! Amen!** *(these words may be sung to a suitable setting)*

The verses of this hymn can be sung progressively through Advent, adding a verse each week as the candles on an Advent Ring are lit.

**Deep in darkness we begin**      **Hymn**

Deep in darkness we begin,
dark outside and deep within.
Now ignite a single flame,
shadows form, let light remain.

As they gleaned the word of life,
narrative of love and strife,
people through each age have known
yet more light: God's glory shown.

John the Baptist spoke out loud,
challenged that discordant crowd,
called each one toward the light,
see it growing, gleaming bright.

Mary wondered at her lot,
blessed? Or cursed? Or loved? Or not?
Angels came and glory shone,
feel the love, let light shine on.

Look! A star is shining there.
See the stable stark and bare.
Christmas dawns, all darkness gone!
Christ has come, the light shines on!

7.7.7.7   Tune: LAUDS (Wilson)

95

# Christmas

Sometimes the significance of what Mary and Joseph were asked to do is not real enough in human terms. It is as if the story of the angels speaking to them blots out the consequences of their acceptance of their roles. These pieces attempt to bring back that reality and to show the human reaction to that commitment.

## Birth pangs

When I said, 'Yes,'
I did not know where it would lead.
Why, in God's name,
must it be here and now?
Why, after all the prejudice I'd known,
the scorn, derision,
and the hostile stares –
why did I have to suffer
this last indignity?
I should have been safe home in Nazareth
with family and warmth
and all the preparations I had made
to have my child in peace.
Now, I must face the fact
this child will wait no longer
and here, among the straw and animals,
with no cradle,
no attendant midwife or family support,
I must bring my first child to birth.
The pain is greater now
and far more frequent,
but, between the spasms,
I can see Joseph's anxious face,
hear the animals move
and wonder why God let the Romans
hold their census at a time like this.
Did he not hear my prayers
that the journey could be postponed
until the child was born safely?
Travelling in my condition,
with only a donkey
and a worried husband
was not the ideal way
to precipitate the birth
of the Son of God.

The pains are stronger now.
My times of lucid thought
shortened by agony beyond belief.
How long will it be now?
Oh, God! When I said, 'Yes!'
How could I have known?

### We see the eyes of Mary shine     Hymn

We see the eyes of Mary shine,
for all the pain of birth is past.
She cradles Jesus in her arms,
her time of joy is here at last.

We see old Joseph's roughened hands,
his eyes are filled with tender joy.
He gently reaches for the child,
this little scrap, this baby boy.

And can they know? And could they guess
at love's responsibility,
that hurt would mingle with the joy
of human possibility?

But on this night a single star
is just enough to signal grace:
a child is born in Bethlehem
and offered for the human race.

LM    Tunes: AMEN SIAKUDUMISA or TRURO

### Who is this baby?

He was not a fairy-tale figure,
     but a living, breathing person.
He was born, not into a privileged home,
     but into a workman's family.
He was born, not into a successful lifestyle,
     but into a community where hard work was the only way to sur
He was born, not in peace,
     but into a world of power struggle and conflict.
He did not remain a baby,
     but grew through years of schooling
     and adolescent questioning into a man with a mission.
He was born, not to be popular with everyone,
     but to make bitter enemies by speaking out about hypocrisy.

97

He was not oblivious to human suffering,
>   but experienced emotion and deprivation
>   and witnessed cruelty
>   and the political manoeuvrings of an unjust society.

He was born, not to live long,
>   but to die too soon, in his thirties.

He was born into a world like ours,
>   but his birth was only the beginning of the story.

Then he grew up.
The experienced, adult Jesus is as concerned with our problems as we are.
Grow along with him and discover that truth.

### Christmas is real      Hymn

Christmas is real when the cost that we measure
reaches the manger and touches the skies,
shop-fronts give way to divine revelation,
God is among us and selfishness dies.

Christmas is real when the gifts that are given
mirror the love of this God upon earth,
God who is known in self-giving and loving,
crowning our poverty, coming to birth.

Christmas still echoed when screams of the children,
slaughtered by Herod inflamed people's fear.
Christmas remains when the trees and the tinsel
make way for news that we'd rather not hear.

Christmas is real when we enter the squalor
mirrored in Bethlehem so long ago;
off'ring the love that was seen in the God-head,
total self-giving, not baubles and show.

11.10.11.10   Tune: EPIPHANY HYMN

**Keep joy alive!**     **Hymn**

Keep joy alive! The angels sing
that peace can come to earth!
The reign of God is heralded,
the Christ has come to birth!

Amid the carolling and food,
the gleaming Christmas lights,
a child was born in poverty,
on this the night of nights.

And as the laughter dies away,
the parties have been cleared,
the world, it seems, remains unchanged,
and hatred is still feared;

until we grasp the central fact
that love is lost and dead
unless we share that love ourselves
and follow where Christ led.

The peace of God will then begin,
and love will come to birth!
Keep joy alive! With angels sing:
God's reign has come to earth!

CM     Tune: KILMARNOCK

# Blue Christmas

*See also 'God go with you' p.22*

It is no coincidence that there are more suicides around Christmas time than at other times of the year. Our expectations of Christmas are rarely met, and if we feel low to begin with what hope is there? We can hide away till it's all over, or we can put on a mask, pretend to be happy, when inside we're falling apart.

It is tempting, in the church, to gloss over these problems. After all, this is a time of celebration. If we do this, we have put our own satisfaction ahead of the needs of people with whom we are called to minister. We become like those who pass by on the other side because we have more important things to do. The alternative is to take these experiences seriously and to recognize that for some people this time is hard and that celebration is not easy.

In some parts of the world an attempt is made formally to minister to people's needs in this situation. This is the idea of a Blue Christmas.

What follows are resources that may be used to share something of the essence of Christmas, acknowledging the needs of those who may have lost children or parents, sisters or brothers; those who have relationship difficulties or broken marriages; those who are in financial difficulty or who are out of work; those who are unwell or terminally ill; alone or depressed.

The following liturgy can be used in its entirety, or single items may be used on their own.

## A liturgy for a blue Christmas

Leader:    It is close to Christmas and for all of us this raises mixed emotions. It is a cliché to say that this time is difficult. But it is. It can be. Some of us have lost children or parents, sisters or brothers. Some of us have relationships that are crumbling, or marriages or partnerships that have broken. And they say this is a time for families.

All around us are signs of wealth and everyone seems to be spending, yet we have no money. Debt cripples us and we see no end to it, but others want us to 'join in'. For some of us work is a memory, or we have been put out of work at just the wrong time, if ever there is a right time.

And how can we celebrate when we are waiting for the results of medical tests, feeling unwell or know that we are terminally ill?

It is easy to feel very alone or depressed.

No one here will make light of this or deny the reality of another's distress. We are here because we need to be here.

What I'm going to ask you to do will be for no one else to see, unless you choose to let them, for no one else to know. Write on a piece of paper, draw if you prefer, something which expresses what you really feel. Swear if you like. Say what you dare not say outside. Let loose your feelings.

*In the quiet, give time for people to write or draw, or simply to sit. When you sense that they have finished, continue.*

Leader:    As we think on what we have written or drawn, let us quietly listen to some music.

*Music should be sensitively chosen, need not be religious and must not have words.*

Leader:    So what is this Christmas?

## This time of tinsel

This time of tinsel hides a paradox.

Homeless and cold, the unmarried mother, the uncertain father, wait. You've heard the story – unreal – shepherds and angels, wise men and imagined camels, an inn and a star. It all added up to a squalid birth in a dirty out-house. No one to turn to, miles from home and soon to be refugees.

Two thousand years on we meet. And it's all meant to be perfect. It never was, it never is, it never will be. That's reality, not some imagined fairy-tale.

When they returned I suppose there were mundane moments, shopping, bartering, making ends meet. This carpenter (was he a master carpenter?) reliant on orders, rushed off his feet one minute, trying to make enough money to live on the next, make do and mend. Tongues wagging at their sometimes strained, strange relationship. Those plaster saints make it all look so idyllic; not quite human; not human at all.

Jesus was nearly 30 when he took that 'adolescent' hike out into the wilderness after hearing his cousin's preaching. If it wasn't for his quiet demeanour, you'd label him fanatical. He was out there for 40 days. I guess his parents worried, perhaps as they had when they'd lost him in the city, in Jerusalem, that time. It doesn't matter how old they grow, they still matter. They are still your children.

And then he was going to set the world to rights. In the end, they got him. Hung him out to dry. And she watched. That was real, blood and nails and that crass crown. Yes, that was real to him, to his parents.

And again, here we are. Still this strange Christmas. We know more now about that story but they keep making it into some cartoon of unreality. Given a chance, we can identify with the search for somewhere to stay, existing hand-to-mouth to try to get a living, the criticism of friends about the way we live our lives. Perhaps we know the grief of losing a child, of watching suffering and being unable to prevent it, of facing an uncertain future.

Yes, now it's you and me. And our story is all too real too.

The tinsel, the baubles, the lights, just heighten our sense of being outside of it all. Just pause for a moment and realize how unreal all that is. Then picture that first Christmas. We're probably nearer the reality of it than any carolling crowd, any supermarket hype, any over-facing feast. For Mary and Joseph, for Jesus, the reality of Christmas and all that followed was grounded in human need, fear, uncertainty.

They believed, though, that God was there with them, not in the palaces with the fortunate, the undisturbed. That's important. God is still here, with you and me. That's the story, theirs and ours. Amen. So be it. Amen.

*Silence*

Leader:      Now hear these words:

Reader:      Remember, says God, I am with you always, to the end of the age.
Your help comes from me, I will not let your foot be moved; I will
not slumber. I will neither slumber nor sleep.
I will keep you from all evil, even that evil, that fear in which you
rest at this moment. I will keep you safe.

Remember that this God will keep you as you come or go.
God will keep you at Christmas and beyond.
From this time on, we can know in our hearts and our minds
that nothing will ever be able to separate us from God's love.
*(adapted from Ps. 121; Matt. 28.20; Rom. 8.39 NRSV)*

Leader:      If you feel that you can, then sing these words with me:

## Awake again within the love      Hymn

Awake again within the love
that lit the stars, that formed the earth,
that ransomed captive Israel
that met us in Messiah's birth:

We praise you, God, our ground of hope,
our source of life and faith and grace.
We reach to you beyond this realm
yet greet you in each other's face.

You are the paradox of power
poured out till love is all that's left:
till ancient fears are met and quelled
and death itself is staunched, bereft.

So, as we face another day,
as hours unfold and hopes are honed,
enlarge our insight of your love,
until our faith is fully grown.

LM    Tune: I SAW THREE SHIPS

Leader:      And now let us mark this moment, that we might remember this
time. Let those who wish to, let go of the paper on which they wrote
or drew. *(a receptacle or a shredder can be available for the paper)* Then
light a candle as a sign that we hope for light even in our darkness,
that we trust that, in Jesus, light has come into the world and that
the darkness has never, will never, put out that light.

*While this takes place music can again be played. This should be sensitively chosen, need not be religious and must not have words.*

And our prayers:

*This point can be marked in silence to allow for personal prayers, or one or more of the following items may be used.*

Leader:    For those who grieve:

## Remembering

Part of your memory
will be rooted in this place –
the time of sorrow
that you thought would never end.

Part of your life
will always be linked
to this pilgrimage –
this remembrance.

Yet now you know
that he/she is carried with you
in the joy of living.

While you live
he/she dances alongside you
and in his/her freedom
you can breathe in
that remembrance
any time,
anywhere.

*Love lives!*

Leader:    For those living with broken love, abused or let down by those
           they trusted:

## Alone

You are alone,
but you will not be alone.
You have been let down,
abused, hurt.

Yet God will ease your pain,
and wait with you in sorrow.

Tomorrow, whenever tomorrow comes,

God will build with you again.
You are more precious to God than you can imagine,
for God loves you
even when you cannot love yourself.

There will be a new tomorrow.
And the pain of today will gradually fade.
The guilt of today will pass.

The light of hope will dawn again
bringing colour back to your life.

*Love lives!*

Leader:      For those in debt:

## Penniless

The ends will never meet
and there are so many 'needs'
and still more 'wants'.

Everyone around seems to have all that they need,
and more.
And you feel despair, for you enter this season of plenty
empty.
All seems hopeless.

Festivity is passing you by.
Soft words don't take away the debt.
The experience of others is not yours.

But you are more valuable to God
than you might anticipate.
Even in your depression and hopelessness
you are worth more
than if you were not here.

God will not leave you.
You will live through this time.
Hold fast to the love that will never let you go
and when your grasp is feeble
remember you are held.

Remember,

*Love lives!*

Leader:     For those who are sick or dying:

## Anxiety never helped

Anxiety never helped,
but anxiety is your watchword.
It must be.
Well, that's how it seems.

All this talk of birth and children;
the noise of play disturbs
and thoughts are of young lives
that you will never see grown.

Life is cruel,
very cruel.
It all seems hopeless
and pointless.
It's not that tomorrow never comes,
it comes too soon
and is filled with dread.

This spiral of depression seems to go all the way down.
Is there no way up?

Those words come back again:
nothing in all creation,
nothing in life or death, St Paul says,
that can separate us from God's love . . .

May you be assured of the truth of these words,
now,
at this very moment,
and in all that the future brings.

Remember,

*Love lives!*

Leader:     And if you can sing it, a hymn to end our time together:

## When fear of what might lie ahead          Hymn

When fear of what might lie ahead
is racing through your mind,
you're held within a greater love,
for God is calm and kind.

When clouds obscure both joy and faith
and hope is coarsely scorned,
a hidden grace of stronger power,
that God has forged, is formed.

Around you there is human love
and human hands to touch,
a person holds you as you weep,
God knows you need as much.

The love in which you're framed and held
will hold when hope has gone,
together in companionship
there's strength to carry on.

And when you come again beyond
the darkness to the light,
that love that held you will not wane
for God will make things right.

CM    Tune: AMAZING GRACE

Leader:     As we depart, greet each other if you can. Know that others are
            bound to you by the time we have shared, will pray with you and
            for you in the coming days. This time will pass. We will come
            through it together. God's steadfast loving-kindness and
            faithfulness can be mirrored in our concern, in genuine love for
            each other.

            Then let us go in peace. Amen. Amen.

*There must be space and time for people to linger long after this liturgy if they need to.*

## Christmas is a family time

The liturgy above is specifically for people who find Christmas difficult for a variety of reasons. What follows can be incorporated into an ordinary act of worship during the pre-Christmas or Christmas season. It could be used with several or a few voices. Parts of it may be omitted, if they seem particularly inappropriate, but do not do this lightly – there may be people present who need to hear expressed something they have never voiced, but that has been a hidden part of their lives.

Christmas is a family time. A time for the gathering of long-lost relatives and excited children. A time for cards and greetings and to celebrate together.

Or is it?

We recognize at this time those people who find it impossible to be a part of family Christmas festivities.

So, we come –

> We who are old and lonely, the last of the family line.
>
> We who are alone unwillingly and have no family contacts.
>
> We who have never been a part of a real family, but have been wandering, we who have been brought up in care, perhaps unable to put down roots in a settled home life.
>
> We who have left the family because of disagreements and have now severed relationships completely.
>
> We who have experienced abuse or violence from the family that should have offered love.
>
> We who have deliberately done what we wanted to do, regardless of the consequences to the rest of the family, and who now feel remorse, but dare not seek forgiveness.
>
> We who have been separated or divorced, and still have family issues to resolve.
>
> We who have not been parented well and whose only solution has been to leave home.
>
> We who have never had children, but have ached for them.
>
> We whose children have chosen the wrong direction in life, and who are now a source of anguish to us.
>
> We who have known the anguish of having children who have died too young.
>
> We who have lost children through miscarriage or stillbirth.
>
> We who have suffered the grief of bereavement and for whom the family is no longer complete.

Father God, though our families are fractured and we feel that we cannot celebrate, remind us that we are all a part of your family and that you hold us in your care, whatever else may be happening in our world.

*Silence*

Give us the courage to face the joy that others have at this time, even though our own hearts are aching and our spirits are low. Hold us safe, Father, until you can bring us through to a place of Christmas hope.

# Holy Week

## On the edge of the action – an order for worship

This is a complete act of worship, although individual items could be lifted out for use elsewhere. A leader will guide the congregation through the order and introduce the characters as they appear. It is helpful if the parts are played by people of approximately the right age. This is especially important with John Mark and his mother, as their roles are interlinked. This is particularly suitable for worshipping 'in the round', as the characters could remain seated, if the gathering is a small one, creating real intimacy – real story-telling.

*The leader, or several people, share the hymns and opening prayers.*

*The following hymn or 'Jesus, donkey-carried treasure' (John Bell/Graham Maule © 1988 WGRG)*

**To bring a city to its sense**     **Hymn**

To bring a city to its sense,
a nation to its knees,
they welcomed Nazareth's carpenter,
waved palms cut from the trees.

Hosannas filled the quiet air,
they strained to glimpse a view;
'Messiah' they acclaimed this man,
that Pharisees would sue.

He turned the tables upside down,
he spun their world around,
he challenged preconceived ideas
flung hatred to the ground.

This man had learnt too much, it seemed,
knew ways of right and wrong,
his ear attuned to righteousness
sensed discord in their song.

The politicians and the priests
were threatened by this choice;
The hypocrites would silence him,
and still we shun his voice.

CM    Tunes: FINGAL or WINCHESTER OLD

**Prayer**

Challenging God, during this Holy Week you face us with many images of Jesus confronting authority and putting himself into dangerous situations. We see him questioning values and condemning hypocrisy, eating and meeting with the most unlikely people and agonizing over his friends and what would happen to them after his death.

The biggest challenge of all was his decision to face the way of the cross. He did not do it willingly, but with a sense of resignation to the inevitable and the knowledge that it was the only way to prove, with finality, that nothing that the power of evil could do could kill your love for us.

As we see the challenges he faced, help us to face our own.

Give us courage to speak out; wisdom to recognize the truth; energy to counter apathy and strength to guide us through suffering.

We do not always understand what you are asking us to do – or why – but teach us to trust and to follow, knowing that death is not the end of the story.

Amen.

**Lord's Prayer**

*The following hymn or 'Can we by searching find out God?'*

**We do not know the reason why**      **Hymn**

We do not know the reason why
you seek us out to set us free;
yet by your words, the way you look,
there is some purpose you can see.

The questions that we dare not ask
are open to your searching eye,
you see through all our doubt, deceit,
exposing each unspoken lie.

In brokenness, yet now secure,
our lives are open to your word,
and every single thing you say
makes all the past seem so absurd.

We struggle then to counter you,
yet argument makes little sense.
We feel amazement at your call.
You break and shatter each defence.

It feels as if you touch each truth,
have walked beside us from our birth,
have taken every sin and stain
and now affirm our human worth.

So every day we'll live for you,
in every way we'll offer praise.
As you have made our lives complete,
so we will serve you all our days!

LM    Tune: NIAGARA

# Holy Week Stories

**Leader:**

Why 'on the edge of the action'?

The pieces you're about to hear are fictionalized accounts of some of the events of Holy Week. They're not fairy stories. Each one of them is based around a character, only one of which is not actually mentioned in the Bible, but was part of a crowd scene. The justification for telling such stories is in John 21.25 – 'Jesus did many other things as well. If every one of them were written down, I suppose that even the whole world would not have room for the books that would be written.'

I want you to meet my narrator. He'll link together all the stories we're going to hear, but I'll put in a word or two, from time to time – and we'll sing a little to exercise our voices.

But now – let the story begin!

**John Mark:**

And have I got a story to tell you?

Well, several stories really – but they're not all mine.

Although one day, when I'm older, I want to go around the world and tell these stories to everyone. I'm already writing some of them down so that I'll remember them.

My name's John, by the way! John Mark.
I get the Mark from my dad.

And I really feel like I'm a part of these stories. These things happened all around me – to people who live in the same street as me.

And I've got three of them here to tell you what happened to them.

All in the same week.
All here in Jerusalem.
And all because of one man – Jesus.

Let's meet my next door but one neighbour.
She can tell you about the first day of that week.

**The watching woman:**

What a day that was!
What a crazy, crowded, laughable day!
You wouldn't believe it unless you'd been there. I've seen many a strange sight at Passover time, but that one topped the lot.

It all began for me early in the morning. I'd made our meal, swept the room and was just chatting at the doorway with my cousin Anna, who lives down the road. We were full of stories of the characters we'd seen pouring into Jerusalem for the feast. They came from towns and villages all over the country – and further. Some of them had been travelling for days. And all the street traders were out and the travelling pedlars and the merchants from far away. Anyone who thought they could make money from crowds – they were all heading in our direction!
But then Anna and I saw a couple of men coming in the end of our street – and they seemed very different from the rest. They weren't family men with wives and children in tow. They weren't traders either. They were definitely men from the countryside. One of them was very big and burly. They could have been fishermen, by the look – and the smell – of them. But whoever they were, they didn't look as if they were on the right street.

They kept on coming towards us, as if they were looking for something. So we kept an eye on them. We wanted to know what they were doing. Perhaps they were up to no good? You never know these days. But they stopped just before they got to us – right outside my neighbour Eli's house. And as they moved forward, I saw that they were going to steal Eli's colt!
Now that young donkey had never been ridden on before. I'm sure that they'd been saving it for some special reason, because no one else had been allowed to touch it. And these two men were untying the rope!

At that point, I rushed forward and shouted at them.
'What do you think you're doing with that animal? It's not yours! Leave it alone!'

Eli obviously heard the row, because he came rushing out.
'It's all right! Don't worry! It's all been arranged!'

And then the two men just spoke a few words that I didn't hear and off they went with the donkey.
I couldn't believe it, but Eli was always a bit odd, so I just raised my hands in despair and thought nothing more of it.

It wasn't long after that when the rumours about the procession started to fly. Now, I like a good parade – and we have had some good ones over the years at the time of Passover. And these days you've got to take excitement where you find it. Especially if most of your life is spent in the house with the kids – like mine is!

So Anna and I gathered the children and made our way to the place outside the city gate where it seemed all the action was about to take place. People in the crowd were already singing and shouting and cheering. They were also totally destroying all the local palm trees by hacking off branches so that they could wave them!

We soon found out why there was so much excitement. Yet another man was about to declare that he was the Messiah – the One Who Would Come.
Well, we've seen that happen before and the fools have always come to a sticky end at the hands of the authorities . . . but why spoil a perfectly good procession with morbid thoughts like that?
Why put a damper on this man's special day? He wouldn't last very long after it! Why spoil it?

So the crowd got worked up and started shouting,
'Hosanna! Save now! Hosanna! Save now!'
After all, there was always the possibility that this really might have been the one who would lead that army to overthrow the Romans.
And they waved their palm branches and threw their coats on the ground and they yelled out that this was the Son of David coming to save them.
If the authorities didn't know about this man already, they certainly found out about him then. You could hear the noise for miles!
We were near the city gate and couldn't see much until the procession was right up to us, but we were just as caught up in the excitement as everyone else.

Well, I was at first! But then I saw the man – nice man, nothing wrong with him – but he was riding – you'll never believe this – he was riding on Eli's donkey! Not a horse, like a proper king would, but a colt – and a borrowed one at that! The coming king – riding on a donkey!

I laughed and I couldn't stop laughing.
What sort of a king is this?
What sort of a Messiah can he be, if he takes that attitude?
What did he think he was doing?
He doesn't stand a chance!

**Leader's comment:**

She's missed the point, hasn't she?
The kind of king who rides on a donkey is the one who comes in peace.
But Jesus was also showing how he was turning worldly values upside down.

His is a topsy-turvy world.
And do you think that we'd have been any better at getting the message than she was?
I don't think so!

Let's sing – verses 1–3 of

### First the cheering    Hymn

First the cheering, then the jeering –
crowds can change their minds at will.
First they hail him, then condemn him;
aim to please, or aim to kill.

First the anger, then the whipping,
clearing out the Temple court.
First the traders, then the money –
space for prayer cannot be bought.

First the perfume, then the poison –
money should not go to waste.
First anointing, then annoyance –
do not judge her deed in haste.

8.7.8.7   Tune: STUTTGART

### John Mark:

I told you she had a good story.
Even if she didn't really understand what Jesus was doing riding that donkey!
But lots of people were like that.

During that week Jesus was always in the news – but always on the move as well.

He upset all the money changers' stalls in the Temple one day – but managed to escape before the authorities caught up with him.

He caused a scandal by having a meal in the house of a man who had been a leper and having perfume poured all over him by a woman.
I need to find out the real details about that.
I'm sure it was harmless.

But Jesus really upset the religious leaders by criticizing them in public and even predicting the downfall of the Temple.

He just didn't seem to care how many enemies he was making.

So, later in the week, that's where my mother's story comes in.

**Mother:**

I'll never forget that night, I can tell you. It's affected the whole of my life ever since then. There's not a chance that I'd ever have been involved with the followers of the Way, if it hadn't been for what happened that night.

In reality, it had all started some weeks before that. Friends who lived in Bethany had come to see me with some very strange stories and a request. They told me about their rabbi friend – the wandering teacher. He was a real character, who didn't care if he offended the other religious people – he even criticized them to their faces!

He just seemed to care about ordinary folk and apparently had a great gift for healing – even when it seemed that the person was dead!

But these friends of mine – another Mary among them; it's far too common a name around here – well, they were beginning to get very concerned that their friend was getting himself into real trouble. He was set on the idea of coming here to Jerusalem to celebrate Passover and they thought that he was heading on a collision course with the authorities.

So they were trying to find him a safe place to celebrate the Passover feast – and they'd thought of my house. Since my husband died I've often earned a little money by letting out the upper room of my house, so they were trying to help me too. My only reservation was when they told me that he would have 12 other friends with him – all men – and most of them from the north, like him. But, as Martha pointed out, the upper room had an outside staircase and once I'd set out the table and bought the food and the lamb for the sacrifice, then they needn't trouble me at all.

In the end, I agreed. And we arranged a secret signal to guide the men to the house without it becoming too obvious. So, on the day that they were to arrive I sent John Mark out with the pitcher for water, at the arranged time. Mark wasn't too pleased about that, I can tell you. Carrying water is work for women and girls, so he was rather embarrassed, to say the least. But it didn't take long and he was soon back, with two men following him into the house. I showed them the room and the provisions and left them to get on with their own preparations.

I was uneasy on the night of the feast. Our family celebration went on as it has for years, but all the time I was conscious that something else was happening in the room above us. It all sounded pretty normal – talking and laughter and quiet pauses when the ceremonial part of the evening was taking place, but at one point it went very quiet and all I could hear was one person moving around the room and the faint splash of water. Then suddenly I heard the voice of big Peter, one of the fishermen. 'No! Not me!' he said really loudly, and then went quiet while Jesus spoke, I think. Then Peter's voice came again, 'Not just my feet, then!' I know what it was about now, but at the time it was very puzzling.

Some time later I heard voices – several of them, all at once – saying 'Is it me?' At first I thought it was some kind of competition and when Judas came sneaking down the stairs shortly afterwards and crept off into the shadows, I thought maybe he'd lost and was walking off in a temper. If I'd known then where he was going, I would have sent Mark to warn the others and Jesus might have escaped.

But I know in my heart, that even if his disciples had managed to get him away then, it wouldn't have made any difference in the end. Jesus knew what was going to happen. I'm just glad that I was able to offer a last chance for him to be close to his friends before the crisis of his arrest and death.

So, when they'd sung their hymn and they came down the stairs to go off to the garden, I stood in the doorway and watched. There was something unusually special about that moment. It had an air of significance that I didn't understand until much later, when Mark came running back to tell me about the soldiers and the arrest.

Now, when I look at my upper room, and the other Christians tell me about how they remember Jesus by re-enacting the things that happened there, I thank God that I was able to play some small part in those major events. And I have become a follower of that brave, charismatic man, too. Who would have thought that the Messiah would use my house for his last supper with his friends?

**Leader's comment:**

John Mark's mother is a little more aware of what's happening, but most of it is only in hindsight. Later, we know that the Christians used to meet in the upper room of her house because it's written in Acts 12.12. Peter has just miraculously escaped from prison and 'As soon as he realized, he went to the house of Mary, the mother of John, whose other name was Mark, where many people had gathered and were praying.'

Whether the Last Supper was really held there we'll never know, but it's not important. We do know that she was part of the early Christian movement. Here again, we have another onlooker on the fringe of those historic events, yet not really understanding what was happening.
As we are – so often!

Let's sing again – verses 4–5 of 'First the cheering'

> First the trusting, then betrayal –
> Judas seeking cash in hand.
> First he loved him, then provoked him,
> daring him to take a stand.

> First the kneeling, then the serving,
> showing deep humility.
> First bread breaking, then wine sharing –
> 'Do this as you think of me.'

**John Mark:**

What my mother didn't know was that I was there for the next part of the story.

You see, when the house was full of visitors – it always was for Passover – I used to sleep up on the roof and that meant that I was directly above the room where Jesus and his friends were celebrating.
I didn't really hear much of the detail of what was going on, but they woke me up when they started to sing their last hymn.
I got up quietly and peered over the edge of the roof as they came out of the room and went down the stairs – all talking and laughing, although one or two of them were yawning.
Maybe they'd had too much wine.

I wanted to see where they were going.

Everybody had talked so much about Jesus, but I hadn't really had the chance to get close – until tonight. So I crept very quietly down the stairs – in my nightshirt – and kept in the shadows while I followed them.

They went straight to one of the gardens on the edge of the city, so it was easy to hide among the trees, but still be close enough to see what was going on. They seemed to be praying – and Jesus went off on his own, on the other side, away from me.

The rest of them fell asleep. Jesus wasn't very pleased when he came back and found them!

But before they could wake up properly, I started to hear noises behind me – and it sounded like a great noisy crowd.
Most of all, it sounded like trouble!

It was!

Leading the crowd was the man I now know as Judas.
All I knew then was that he was supposed to be a friend of Jesus.
He looked like a friend – when he went to him and kissed him.

But that must have been a signal, because suddenly a group of men with clubs and sticks went forward and arrested Jesus in the name of the chief priests and elders.

Then it was complete chaos!

One of the disciples tried fighting them off and I think someone got injured, but I was so frightened that all I wanted to do was to get away.

Just as I started running, somebody grabbed me.

But I was terrified and I fought back.
Luckily he'd only got hold of my nightshirt, not me, and it tore in his hands.
Quick as a flash, I tore it completely and ran for my life.
It never occurred to me that I was running through the streets naked.

But it was dark and I knew all the back alleyways, so I was soon home safely and mother was wrapping a blanket around me and asking what on earth was going on.

I don't know whether I'll ever dare to tell the truth about what happened to me that night.


**Leader's comment:**

He really did tell the truth about it one day.

It's fairly certain that John Mark was the young man whose story is told in the fourteenth chapter of Mark's Gospel. Read it for yourself in verses 50–52.

And it's very likely that he told the story to Peter and Peter urged him to write it down. After all, Peter had his own story of deserting and denying Jesus.


**John Mark:**

Someone else knew one of the things that happened next.

Sarah lives next door and works in the house of the High Priest.

She'll tell you the next part of the story.


**The girl:**

I knew he was one of them!
I knew from the first minute I saw him – sneaking through the gateway like that! Keeping in the shadows. Avoiding people. Trying to cover his face.
It was very easy to see who he was.

I know most of the faces around here.
All the officials – I see them all the time. And the hangers-on – the ones who want to keep in with the authorities. The ones who like to think they're a cut above the rest of us. I see them all the time.
And they all treat me as if I'm invisible.
I'm just a girl. Just a servant. No importance whatsoever. There to be ignored.

117

What they don't realize is that I notice things. We all do – us 'servant' girls. And they don't recognize how much we see, either – or that we understand what's going on. Sometimes the hypocrisy is unbelievable! And these people are supposed to be the leaders, religious leaders at that!
The tales I could tell you . . . but that's not the point!

I was telling you about this man. You know it was the night of the big so-called 'trial', when they'd dragged that carpenter in front of them and he caused such a scandal by claiming to be the Christ.

This other man was terrified. You could see that in his face. That's why he'd kept to the shadows and tried not to be noticed. But it was a cold night, that night, and he must have been frozen with fear as well. So he gradually started moving towards the fire to warm himself.

It was just curiosity on my part, really. In a way I felt sorry for him, because I'm sure his friend wasn't the dangerous rebel they were accusing him of being. So I only went a bit closer to see if I was right about this stranger.

At first he didn't take too much notice of me, although he did turn away when I tried to look straight at him. So I moved around to where I could see him properly and said, 'Weren't you with that Nazarene? That Jesus?'
I didn't really mean any harm by it, but he turned on me as if I was accusing him of a crime and snapped back that he'd had nothing to do with him.

Well, I wasn't out to cause trouble, so I left it and the man disappeared for a while – went over to the gateway, I think. I was out there later myself and I said something about him to the group that was standing around. 'You know, I'm sure that man was with that Jesus.'
He heard me. Probably recognized that I'd said something to him before. And he turned on me again and said, 'No!' but much more forcibly this time. He probably knew that the others were now curious too.

I walked away then. I hadn't really intended to get him into trouble, so I kept out of it. But the word had spread and one of the men went over to accuse him: 'You're a Galilean! You must be a follower!'

Well, you should have heard the language! He was obviously from Galilee – and most likely a fisherman, judging by some of the words he used!
He cursed and swore. He was so angry and so afraid. 'I don't even know this man you're talking about,' he shouted – so loud that heads were beginning to turn – even away from the scene of the trial.

And then the strangest thing happened.
The rooster crowed – and the man stopped shouting and stood stock-still. You'd have thought he'd been struck dumb.

I couldn't understand it.

Dawn was breaking. The rooster was crowing. That's nature for you!
But there was something very significant about it for him.

He seemed to be first terrified, then absolutely devastated.
And, without thinking, I turned to look at the prisoner, Jesus.
He was looking straight at his friend. And there was such sadness in his eyes.
You'd almost think that he was weeping.
And the man, this stranger, just took to his heels and ran, with tears streaming down his face.

I've never seen him since.
But I was right! I knew I'd been right from the start.
He was a follower. Somebody told me later that his name was Simon Peter.

I don't blame him for being afraid. I would have been afraid if I'd been him in that crowd.
But I don't think that I'll ever forget the look that the prisoner gave him.
Because Jesus couldn't possibly have heard what happened, but his look very clearly said, 'I told you what you'd do – even though you said you wouldn't!'

And how do you live with yourself, when you've betrayed your friend like that?

### Leader's comment:

How *do* you live with yourself when you've betrayed your friend like that?
Would we have been any better? Alone in a hostile crowd – frightened – terrified on your friend's behalf – not wanting to do or say anything that would make things worse? And feeling so helpless.
How would we have reacted?

Let's sing again – verse 6 of 'First the cheering'

> First the garden, then the praying –
> sweating blood, then traitor's kiss.
> First the trial, then denial –
> Peter, has it come to this?

### John Mark:

The rest of the story is all about the way they killed Jesus – and we'll have to leave that for another day.

But I'll never forget what happened that week.
Neither will the others.
We may just have been spectators – only on the fringe of the action – but we've never been the same since.

That's what getting involved with Jesus does to you!

It changes your life.

Thank you for listening.

**Leader's comment:**

But listening isn't enough.
Getting involved with Jesus changes lives.
As we move further into the week when we remember the suffering and death of Jesus, let us be more than spectators on the fringe of the action. Let us enter that upside-down world of active love that Jesus showed, by being prepared to go to the limits to identify with people.

Let's sing the last two verses of that hymn, 'First the cheering'

> First the nails and then the hammer
> piercing flesh and splitting bone.
> First the sighing, then the dying –
> Jesus on the cross, alone.

> First the grieving, then the praying,
> agonizing through your death.
> First we share your desolation –
> while you wait to take new breath.

Let's just be quiet for a while.

*Silence*

As we continue our journey through Holy Week let us pray:

Lord, we recognize that far too often we remain on the edge of the action, reluctant to be involved in your suffering as we see it in your people.
Help us to conquer our fears,
to acknowledge our failings,
to ask forgiveness for our wrongs
and grant us courage to continue on this road,
walking alongside you in the way of the cross.

So –
Joy be with us to take to those in sorrow.
Peace be with us to take to those in trouble.
Love be with us to take to those whose lives are empty.
God be with us to take our hands
and guide us in God's work.
**Amen.**

And for those times when there is a Communion service during Holy Week, this act of worship tries to make the scene vivid and alive. Much of this material could be used at other times of the year.

## Holy Week Communion

**Call to worship**

**Worship God with all your being**
Worship God with all your being:
God transcendent, in this place!
Glancing, shifting, dancing spirit,
immanent, the source of grace.
Face to face with God we honour
values that the Christ would crown,
we would risk divine communion,
see the world turned upside down.

*The following hymn or 'First the cheering' starting at p.113 in this book)*

**Rising gloom surrounds the story**       **Hymn**
Rising gloom surrounds the story,
Jesus moves towards the cross,
here Jerusalem is waiting,
favour swings from gain to loss.

Crowds had swarmed in adulation,
others came infused with hope.
Every person sought an outcome,
nothing seemed beyond his scope.

Zealots called for liberation,
sinners waited on his word,
children ran with palms to meet him,
felt affirmed by what they heard.

Other people simply bustled,
hardly noticed his approach
riding humbly on a donkey,
thought their lives beyond reproach.

In the temple, tables turning,
those in power were disabused
as he showed the way to worship
for the poor, despised, abused.

Choices faced him in the garden,
prayer was dry, betrayal lurked;
while his closest friends were sleeping
human evil waited, worked.

What is left? Some trumped-up charges,
self-conceit, religious hate?
Here the Christ still stands before us –
time for judgement . . . crosses wait.

8.7.8.7   Tunes: ADORATION (Hunt) or GALILEE

*Reading Jn. 2.13–22 (NRSV)*

### Love inspired the anger       Hymn

Love inspired the anger
that cleared a temple court,
overturned the wisdom
which their greed had wrought.

Love inspired the anger
that set the leper free
from the legal strictures
that brought misery.

Love inspired the anger
that cursed a viper's brood:
set on domination,
self with God confused.

Love inspires the anger
that curses poverty,
preaches life's enrichment,
seeks equality.

Love inspires the anger
that still can set us free
from the world's conventions
bringing liberty.

6.6.6.5   Tune: NORTH COATES

## The Peace

There was anger.
There still is.
But we come in peace
Let us offer a sign of that peace to each other.

## Earth-maker      Hymn

Earth-maker, source of the world and our wisdom,
lover and carer, forever the same.
Bread for our sustenance, all we have needed,
you offer freely, we worship your name.

Pain-bearer, holding the fragile and faulted,
loving the broken and tending the frail;
bringing forgiveness and grace for our mending,
you are the heaven where love will not fail.

Life-giver, offering justice and mercy,
needing your presence we come at your call;
hallow your name through the whole of creation,
you reign in glory for ever and all!

11.10.11.10   Tunes: EPIPHANY HYMN or STEWARDSHIP

## The Lord's Supper - Thanksgiving

### Narrator:

Thirteen men met round the table that evening, ready to celebrate the memory of one great historical break for freedom. They were excited and full of the events of the week in the city, laughing and talking and exchanging stories. Only two of them knew that the night would end with a betrayal that would lead to tragedy.

What a collection of men they were! Several tough, argumentative, forthright, north country fishermen, a tax collector, a fervent Jewish nationalist, a couple who were concerned with money – one about overspending, one about acquiring more – another who was never very sure of himself, or of anyone else, and several who kept their heads down and seemed to be content to be background figures.

The conversation and the wine flowed freely and for most of the men it seemed like any other Passover feast. Occasionally someone asked Jesus a question and the room quietened while he answered. One or two of them had private words with him, but that was not unusual, some had always been in a kind of inner circle.

But no one took much notice of the fact that Judas was acting even more strangely than ever, jumpy and nervous and very aware of the time they were taking with the meal. He had always kept himself slightly apart from the others and was sometimes critical of the way Jesus behaved, so he was not the most popular member of the group. Perhaps that is why no one could really remember when he left the room. The rest of them carried on talking and waited to see what Jesus wanted to do next.

When the supper was finished, there was a break in the conversation.

In the sudden silence, Jesus picked up bread and broke it in pieces.

Jesus:     This bread is my body and I am broken for you and others like you. Take a piece, each of you, and eat it.

Narrator:   As they did that, he lifted the cup of wine.

Jesus:     Blood,

Narrator:   he said

Jesus:     my blood. I'll be spilling it for you and for everyone else. Drink, please, all of you.

Narrator:   They didn't understand the significance of what he said, but they did as he asked.

Jesus:     You'll never forget this night,

Narrator:   he said.

Jesus:     Each time you break bread and drink wine, you'll remember me.

Narrator:   He was right. They did remember – and, even today, so do we, as we break bread and drink wine together.

## The Breaking of the Bread

When we break bread we share in the Body of Christ.
For though we are many, we are one.

## The Sharing of the Bread and Wine

## The story stands, a memory remains        Hymn

The story stands, a memory remains:
that night of crisis, time of chance and choice;
prefigurement of death, eternal gains,
a time to meet with fear, or to rejoice.

That tangled gang of misbegotten men
had gathered with their master for a meal.
Through Passover they celebrate again,
his words were enigmatic, stark, yet real.

The wine was wine, the bread was only bread.
What was that talk of body and of blood?
They strained to understand the things he said,
make sense of  every symbol as they should.

Yet, if the meal we share is more than act,
a play with words, mere taste of bread and wine,
then we must demonstrate the living fact
that love is always part of God's design.

10.10.10.10   Tune: WOODLANDS


## Prayers

We have not forgotten that night, Lord.
Together we have remembered it and remembered your sacrifice.
Those men were changed by their experience
and we are too.
Help us to demonstrate the living fact
that sacrificial  love is always part of your design.

*Extempore intercessory prayers may be offered at this point*


## Jesus the carpenter, hanging on Calvary   Hymn

*Jesus the carpenter, hanging on Calvary,*
*nails through your feet and your work-hardened hands –*
*wood you have worked with and wood is your destiny –*
*paying the price of our sinful demands.*

You came to our world as a part of a family,
living and learning the carpenter's trade.
You followed your father's instructions so faithfully,
shaping and crafting the yokes that you made:

   *Chorus*

You called other workmen to join in your ministry,
laying rough hands on the sick and the lame.
You taught of God's love with such power and authority,
people who knew you believed you insane:

   *Chorus*

You faced with great courage the open hostility
coming from those who believed they were right.
They stripped you and beat you and laughed at you finally,
thinking your death was the end of the fight:

   *Chorus*

But we, who now know that you ended triumphantly
working with wood till your task was complete,
can come to your cross with our hope and humility,
laying our pride at the carpenter's feet:

> *Chorus*

13.10.13.10 and chorus    Tune: BLOW THE WIND SOUTHERLY

## Blessing

From a stall in a stable to a cross on a hill wood was your way of life, Christ
the carpenter. Bless us now in our lives that whatever our destiny we will walk
the way to it with the same courage and determination as you had. Amen.

# Good Friday

Good Friday is a cruel day and we must face that reality. These pieces reflect
the agony.

## Tortured, beaten, scarred and tainted

Tortured, beaten, scarred and tainted,
not a picture deftly painted,
more a tattered, battered being,
torn, disfigured, stark, unseeing.

Muscles twisted, strained, contorted,
body dangling, bruised, distorted.
Life blood drying, sun-baked, stinging,
hatred, bitter hatred, flinging.

Crowds insensate, tempers vented,
full of anger, discontented.
Curses scattered, insults flying,
spurned, derided, God is dying.

## The wondrous cross

'When I survey the wondrous cross'. That's what they sang, and I was with
them; have been with them over the years; on a hillside, in many a chapel and
church, in a town square with all the people milling around; people curious,
not understanding. And in the church, the preacher said it was all part of
God's plan.

And I cast my imagination back over millennia 'outside a city wall', and it doesn't seem wondrous at all. At best it is grotesque or sordid, at worst gruesome, foul, horrific; nailed flesh and the screams of the dying. And it is so hard to make sense of this; more vindictive than redemptive.

And we cover it with layers of sentiment, we cloak it with beauty, we smother the reality of the horror with soft words. All this can so easily be sweetened with Easter eggs and beautified with flowers.

What does it all mean? Dear God, what does it all mean?
Nothing, save God is here.

But that's it, I suppose, and a grim reminder that we maim and kill for political reasons, for religious reasons, out of expediency; that the world hasn't changed in all those 2,000 years. 'A time for birth and a time for death' rings down the ages. And still we stand at the foot of a cross. And still we condone the violence that it pictures. And still we wonder:

'God, when will it end?
When will you breathe love into OUR lives?
When will we ever learn?'
And in the church the preacher says it is all part of God's plan.

## Each groan of pain from tortured lips     Hymn

Each groan of pain from tortured lips,
each tear that falls from anguished eyes,
the slightest murmur of a sigh,
as yet another victim dies,
are nails into the hands of Christ
counting against the tyrant's lies.

Each agony of starving death,
each haunted look of gaunt despair,
the scrabbling hands that search the dirt
although the earth is cracked and bare,
are echoes in the mind of Christ
of his last agonizing prayer.

Each home destroyed by missile blast,
each terror of a war-torn land,
the crying of a frightened child,
alone without a loving hand,
are spears pierced in the side of Christ
and pain which he can understand.

Each empty mind, which sees no pain,
each ignorance of crying need,
the pleas of those who go unheard,
while others wallow in their greed,
are thorns upon the brow of Christ
and open wounds that tear and bleed.

Each healing touch relieving pain,
each voice, which speaks aloud for peace,
the giving hearts and willing hands,
working so poverty may cease,
are living out the words of Christ,
striving to give his love release.

8.8.8.8.8.8   Tune: ABINGDON (an alternative tune: BANNERMAN by Paul Bateman is available from Stainer & Bell Ltd.)


## Agony

Agony etched on faces.
Pain screaming from tortured limbs.
Blood running from open wounds, mingling with sweat, diluted by tears.
Victims dying.
Soldiers doing their duty.
Enemies looking on with hatred blazing.
Mothers weeping inconsolably.
Friends standing, lost and helpless, at a distance.

No solution.
Only the tearing last breath as death puts an end to it all.

Dear God,
how many times have such scenes been witnessed?
How many times have we wept for the agony of another's pain?
How often have we prayed for the end of another conflict?
How often have we been aware of cruel torture inflicted by vindictive power?
How often have we had to stand helplessly at a distance, believing nothing can be done?
How often have we despaired when death appears to have the final victory?

Yet, on that cross,
on that day,
there was total identification with the agony of the world.

God, help us,
in our darkest hours,
to remember that.

# Easter

The resurrection is a blazing certainty to many Christians, but that assurance can be a stumbling block to people who cannot understand the mystery, or have doubts about the details of the stories. We have no right to condemn this attitude. There was a great deal of uncertainty around on the days following the death of Jesus and different people had to come to understanding in their own time and in their own way. Admitting that this issue is not an easy one to deal with can open a door to faith to those who can be put off by uncompromising certainty.

### I have a picture in my mind . . .

I have a picture in my mind of a churchyard. Serried ranks of graves stretch into the distance. Some are upright like the military men I imagine them commemorating. Others seem to be tossed on a sea of turf, a veritable field-day for a health and safety executive, yet they remain from year to year.

In the distance I see a new eruption of soil, fresh and moist. The flowers, that two days before had been so carefully placed on this new grave, have been cast aside. My footsteps quicken. My feelings are not of joy, rather of fear and anger.

Sacrilege! Who could do this? And where is the coffin now? And I want to shout and cry all at once. What has happened?

'And on the first day of the week they came to the tomb wondering between themselves who would roll away the stone from the entrance. And when they looked up, they saw that the stone, which was very large, had already been rolled back'.

No stone, no Jesus, no Christ! No alleluia either! Just startled fear.

'So they went out and fled from the tomb, for terror and amazement had seized them; and they said nothing to anyone, for they were afraid.'
(based on Mk. 16.2-4, 8).

It was only much later, some say later that day, when it began to make sense. And for some it still doesn't make sense. An empty tomb doesn't prove resurrection. And the sense of a dead person 'being around' doesn't either. I remember my father walking up a churchyard with me once. He'd never been there and had been dead for nearly 10 years. But I was sure he was there.

No. Something stronger changed those fearful women and frightened men, something intangible that perhaps we will never touch with our intellect or explain with our knowledge. I have seen lives changed for the better after a death. I have known people turned around by the challenge to their own mortality. And the change is permanent.

What changed the disciples had the potential to change the world. And when we are willing to act like Jesus, IT WILL!

### No soldiers and no body      Hymn

No soldiers and no body,
an empty linen shroud
and women with a story
they dare not tell aloud.
So, put away the spices
intended for the dead
and wait with fear, as they did,
to see some way ahead.

And did the story end there,
the last words torn away?
No final resolution?
What happened on that day?
What changed the gloom to glory?
What cancelled out their loss?
How could there be a victory
beyond that bloody cross?

Before the day had ended
the rumours ran around
that Jesus was still living,
no body could be found.
Authorities denied it,
said that the guards had fled,
but they feared most the story
'He's risen from the dead.'

7.6.7.6.D    Tune: SALLEY GARDENS

### They ran away

'They ran away and said nothing to anyone for they were afraid.'

Would we have reacted any differently?
Would we have been able to take it in?
The unthinkable had happened.
After such a cruel death, after such horror, now they found that they couldn't

even pay their last respects to Jesus because the body had gone.
What had happened?
Surely it couldn't be that he was living again?

Understanding God,
you recognized the fear and bewilderment experienced by those women.
You forgave them their misunderstanding.
You gave them time to take in the possibility that hope was not dead, that life would go on.

We often struggle with our belief too.
Sometimes life defeats us, or death seems so final
and hope is obliterated by fear and anxiety.
Help us to reflect and remember that death was not the end of your story.
From the bewildering events of the resurrection stories, teach us that nothing can ever separate us from your love.
Show us how,
even from darkest death,
life can break through again.

## Come in the morning      Hymn

*Come in the morning.*
*Come see the dawning.*
*Come to the garden –*
*life has broken through.*

Jesus, dead and buried.
To his grave they hurried.
Anxious women found that
life had broken through.

*Chorus*

Soldiers could not keep him
for they were found sleeping
and the tomb was open –
life had broken through.

*Chorus*

Peter, unbelieving,
left, still full of grieving.
Nothing would convince him
life had broken through.

*Chorus*

Mary, greatly shaken,
thought he had been taken.
Heard his voice that told her
life had broken through.

*Chorus*

Where there was despairing,
grief and horror sharing,
now there is a rumour
life has broken through.

*Chorus*

So God's word is spoken,
when our hearts are broken
there will come a time when
new life will break through.

*Chorus*

6. 6. 6. 5 and chorus 5. 5. 5. 5
Tune: DANCE TO THI' DADDY
(When the boat comes in)

And doubt can lead us on to reassurance.

## From the hilltop across the sea

From the hilltop across the sea
light is beginning to colour creation.
Dawn creeps up on us in these latitudes,
a calm caress to a sleeping world . . .

But dawn does not bring life.

At this Easter, O God, give us faith
**to see the light that brings life to humanity.**
Give us hope
**that there is more to life than our present experience.**
Give us love to share
**that is stronger than death.**
Give us peace
**such as the world cannot give.**

Then in our hearts
may alleluias rise and ring.
Be in us with your joy, O God,
**that our joy may be full!**

**Alleluia! Alleluia! Alleluia!**

## Spilling sunshine, love and laughter     Hymn

Spilling sunshine, love and laughter,
Christ will live, death can't destroy.
On the resurrection morning,
all the world will dance with joy.

Symbols sign our exaltation,
crosses decked with springtime flowers,
wine is drunk and bread is broken,
all the grace of God is ours.

Join the throng and sing God's praises;
Alleluias ring the earth!
Alleluia! Praise the Godhead,
source of love and hope's rebirth.

8.7.8.7   Tunes: SHIPSTON or WELLESLEY

# Pentecost

Few strangers visit the church at Pentecost. Some church members avoid it too. Perhaps this is the time when we need material to explain the mysteries to those inside the church who are happy to side-step the commemoration of the power of the Holy Spirit pouring over the believers on that first Christian Pentecost.

We had been singing 'Be still, for the power of the Lord is moving in this place'. Looking around the church there seemed to be little evidence to support the words. I started to scribble on the notice sheet . . .

**Power**

Power, Lord?
Your power?
Moving here?
In this place?

What power?
Where?
Should we expect to see it?

I don't think so!
Can't see much evidence.
People here seem half-asleep.
Old and weary,
solemn and dispirited.

Dispirited?
Is that the clue?
No spirit.
So,
no stirring of the heart.
No impetus to love.
No energy.

We are too still.

Help us to switch into
the current of your power,
so that the real moving can begin.

Your power.
Moving in this place
through us.

In Acts 2 we read of the Spirit coming to the disciples at Pentecost. Before this they had been too frightened to make much of what they had seen and heard while they had been with Jesus.

## Safe, locked inside that upper room     Hymn

Safe, locked inside that upper room,
too scared to let the truth be known,
disciples had to see their Lord
before that truth could be their own.

And Thomas, still so full of doubt,
would not believe the tales they told
till Christ appeared, to show his wounds –
then his conviction made him bold.

Yet doubts and fears returned again.
Once more they locked themselves away
until the Holy Spirit came
on that inspiring, vital day.

The truth is now a living fact.
The love of God can never die.
So bold apostles stood their ground –
their living Lord is not a lie.

We have not seen, but we believe
and we must witness by our faith
to living truth we have received,
awakened by the Spirit's breath.

LM   Tune: NIAGARA

## Strange tongues

I cannot read music.
Those lines and dots
and strangely curving symbols
are merely patterns
filling up a page.

I cannot play music.
Black and white keyboards,
stringed instruments
and tubes of wood, or brass,
are dead in my hands,
silent to my lips.

I cannot sing music –
not with any confidence.
My lips frame words.
My voice sounds tuneless
to my own ears
and I am wary
of letting others hear
my faltering efforts.

Music is a foreign language to me.
And I am as incompetent in that
as I am in other tongues.

Yet music moves my soul
and I listen and am carried
by its haunting power
into a world, alive and beautiful,
and the music speaks
in a voice all its own.

The Spirit's language
is a foreign tongue,
not understood.
And yet it speaks,
controls and liberates
and moves
into the deepest areas of the soul
to make a moving music
of its own.

### Pentecost prayer

Lord, your first followers shut themselves tightly into a room to wait for the coming of your Spirit.

They were afraid of mockery, of persecution and the danger of having to follow you to the cross.

But when your Spirit came, the wind was strong and blew away their doubts.
It refreshed and invigorated them.
It blew them out of their locked room.

The fire of your Spirit rested on their heads, to confirm their commitment and blazed in their hearts to set them alight for you.

So, driven by the wind and lit by the fire, they spilled out into the world to speak the languages of your love.

Dear God, so often we confine ourselves within four walls because we are so afraid of the world outside.
We hear your call to follow in the footsteps of Jesus, but we are not sure we can go so far.

Break through into our lives with your cleansing, driving wind and help us to be willing to be carried along in that power, outside the confines of our safe and secure walls.

Fire our hearts again with the flame of your love, so that we may have a burning desire to reach out to others in your name.

Teach us the language of love that confirms our knowledge of you and speaks to the hearts of all the peoples of your family.

Come, Holy Spirit, come.
Change us and set us free.

## Energy

Energy!
From that Pentecost day.
Pure, unadulterated energy.

The sound of driving wind
bent us to our knees.
We could not stand against it.

The flames burned light and heat
into a coronet of confirmation.

We could not be quiet.
We were babbling
and bubbling over with words and
news.
No wonder they assumed
that we were drunk.

We felt it too.

Drunk with energy,
enthusiasm and power –
after bewildering days
when stories circled
and doubt curled round their edges.
We had not known, as we gathered,
what to expect.
Liberation was so swift.

But now,
we really can do anything,
not just by name,
but also with his power.

He has returned
as Spirit burning and burdening our
hearts.

Pentecost has new dimensions now.
Energy!
Driving energy!

## Inspiration

I hate balloons!
Ever since that day
one horrid child
burst one behind me
at a party,
when I was only four,
or thereabouts –
I've hated balloons.

And yet . . .

a street-seller
captivates children –
and me –
by making shapes and animals,
as he breathes life
into long, thin balloons
and curves and twists them
in his hands.
Then, suddenly, a dog!
And a delighted child
sees, not breath encased,
only a new friend
to carry home with glee.

Empty,
balloons are nothing.
Air-filled,
they live.

Come, Holy Spirit,
pour new life into me,
that I may fill
and change
and live and grow,
transformed
by the very breath of God.

## Wind of the Spirit      Hymn

Wind of the Spirit, move us on,
drive us before your force.
We need that power to strengthen us
of which you are the source.
Blow off the cobwebs of the past
and set us on your course:

> *O come Holy Spirit, move us on,*
> *move us on.*
> *O come Holy Spirit, move us on.*

Fire of the Spirit, burn in us,
surround us with your light.
Destroy our sense of apathy,
give us the will to fight.
That with our hearts on fire for Christ
we set the world alight:

> *Chorus*

Voice of the Spirit speak to us,
give us your words to say.
Inspire the language of your love,
help us to preach and pray.
That all may hear of saving grace
translated for their day:

> *Chorus*

Christ, let your Spirit sweep through us,
your serving church renew.
Give us new hope and confidence
in all the work we do.
That those who seek for faith today
may find their way to you:

> *Chorus*

8.6.8.6.8.6 & Refrain
Tune: GOD REST YOU MERRY

# Celebrating Creation

As well as the recognized pattern of the church year, other seasons of the calendar bring beauty and wonder, a prompt to reflect on God and creation.

**Sensitive God**

Sensitive God,
conductor of musical birdsong,
painter of cloud shapes and sunsets,
planter of pine-scented forests,
grower of mouth-watering melons,
unfurler of soft, silky rose petals,
awaken all our senses to the variety and extravagance of your world.

As we rejoice in the many ways we can see, hear, smell, taste and touch your creation, make us also aware of those who lack one or more of these senses. Lead us, caring God, to the discovery of sensitive ways in which we can help all your children to enjoy the beauty and variety which you have provided for us.

**God has daubed the hills with colour     Hymn**

God has daubed the hills with colour,
painted brilliant azure skies,
offered blinding crimson sunsets
where we feast our longing eyes.
God has offered silence, stillness,
in the quiet of this place,
brought our lives divine renewal
through perceptive, loving grace.

God has brought us closer friendship,
taught us how to laugh and speak,
in a singing, gracious language
sonorous, sublime, unique.
God has bonded us together,
made us one in mind and heart.
As we shared through this endeavour
we are one as we depart.

8.7.8.7.D   Tune: HYFRYDOL

## Harvest

At harvest, many churches have a tradition of bringing baskets of produce as a token offering of the harvest.

### Bring your baskets

Bring your baskets,
tokens of all that you have
and all that you are.

Bring your gifts on this festival day,
be they sheaves of corn
or lumps of coal,
computer chips
or the smiling faces of children that
you teach.*

Bring all that you can,
all that you have,
all that you are.

Bring your prayers for the poor
and your love for the lost.

Without your gifts,
without you,
this world, God's world, is lacking.

**These are our gifts, O God,
which we bring to you in gratitude
and thanksgiving.**

*other specific gifts could be added
at this point.*

### Great God of all creation
#### Hymn

Great God of all creation,
bright as the morning sun,
our dawning praise is rising,
our daily work begun.
A quiet blade is growing,
up from the rich, dark earth,
the life that once was hidden
is springing into birth.

The land is always changing,
it bears our human mark,
idyllic scenes are hiding
a life that's hard and stark.
A lack of understanding
of all we do and share,
obscures the deprivation
that's hardly hidden there.

We work within the compass
that nature will allow,
we follow through the seasons,
we harrow, seed or plough.
O holy one of heaven,
as stewards, give us grace,
to care for your creation,
to value country space.

7.6.7.6.D   Tune: AURELIA

## Thanksgiving

This reflection and the prayers that follow it may be used in a Harvest Festival where there is a traditional display of produce, or in a situation where the display is more sparse, but there is an intention to reconnect with concept of Harvest Thanksgiving.

Remember the smell of Harvest Festival?
The rioting scents of fruit and flowers;
the earthy reality of potatoes and cabbages;
the savoury-sharp catch of breath from onions and leeks;
tomatoes ripening on window ledges
and apples and oranges topped with grapes
and gift-wrapped for later sale?

Just open the door of the church
and open yourself to sight and scent and senses!

Tinned food parcels and bagged sugar,
though given with best intent,
cannot recreate that instant link
with the harvest of the soil –
for the closest contact with earth
that most of us make is with plant pots,
or garden mowers.

But in our time,
with pre-washed, pre-packed, plastic-wrapped produce
travelling from shelf to trolley to car to plate
with hardly a human hand to help,
why should we wonder that harvest means so little,
except where we hear that crops have failed
and respond to the hunger that we see in starving faces?

Perhaps we need to scent the harvest again,
absorb its beauty, inhale the reality,
remember the roots of celebration,
return to the source of our thanksgiving.

Now in this place, at this time let us give thanks.

*Bidding prayers follow which, depending on the situation, will either have the form 'Look around you and give thanks . . .' or 'Now imagine and give thanks . . .'*

Look around you and give thanks (Now imagine and give thanks) for those fruits of harvest which bring memories of celebration.
*Silence*

For these fruits, **we give thanks, O God.**

Those fruits of harvest which taste the best to you
*Silence*

For these fruits, **we give thanks, O God.**

Those things which have the greatest beauty, provoke the greatest sense of wonder.
*Silence*

For these things, **we give thanks, O God.**

Lastly, for what you see or imagine that brings the greatest joy in your life, give thanks.
*Silence*

For all these gifts, **we give you thanks, O God.**
**Amen.**


## Autumn

Autumn is a blazing time,
a red and gold amazing time.
Trees maturing now display
fruit and leaf in fine array.
Trees prepared for winter's rest
show their glories at their best.

Autumn is a dying time,
a withering and a drying time.
Falling leaves are brittle rust
tumbling down into the dust.
Fallen leaves go back to earth,
re-absorbed to bring new birth.

Autumn is a blessing time,
a God-will-keep-us-guessing time.
Emptying branches seem so stark,
stripped to bare and simple bark.
Empty branches on them bear
sleeping buds to wake next year.

So, what about the other seasons?

## Winter

Winter has a dreary sound to it.
Fog, frost, snow, rain and icy winds
all feature heavily.
They turn us indoors
to layers of warm clothing
and firesides and hot drinks,
which are all blessings in themselves.

But on bright winter days
there are unexpected joys.
Sunshine on snow.
Sparkling frosty air.
Tree outlines silhouetted by clear blue sky.
And piercing through the hardened soil
the sharp green points of new life.

We know it will always happen,
but it is good to see
God blessing us, once again,
with his promise of resurrection.

## Spring

Spring is full of energy –
like its name.
It coils and tenses and waits
and then jumps out at us,
bursting with vigour
and new life
and shouts its presence
with a this-is-what-you've-been-waiting-for attitude.

Spring blesses us in an aggressive way.
Bare trees suddenly thrusting out new leaves.
Flowers shaking their defiant colours,
even at the occasional return of wintry weather.
Animals and birds proudly parade young ones.
Lawns and hedges cry out for mowers and trimmers.
And the sun gains strength and length of days
and by its energy
urges us to get out and do something.

Energetic God,
we thank you for the urgent message of renewal
that blesses us with each spring.

## Summer

Summer is extravagant
and over-stated
and showy.

Summer colours are bright
and gaudy
and over-the-top.

Summer life is abundant
and prolific
and overwhelming.

Summer sun is dazzling
and brilliant
and hot –

sometimes.

Summer rain is warmer,
but just as wet
as at any other time.

Yet summer riots its colours loudest
where sun and showers combine
to bring out the glory.

Just as God's blessings abound
in the joy and sorrow
by which all growth comes.

# BLESSINGS

Judging by the number of small cards sold in Christian bookshops there is a great demand for a simple message of blessing to be given to those in need or trouble. Even those who would claim to have no religious faith welcome words of comfort, or encouragement, or love, at certain times in their lives – even on a daily basis. A surprising number of inspirational cards can be found tucked into the wallets, purses or books of the most unexpected people. They even find their way onto pin boards and notice boards in all kinds of work places and homes.

## Greet each new day with hope

Greet each new day with hope.
Live each new day with courage.
Share each new day with others.
End each new day with prayer.
Sleep and peace will bless you.

### As the day dawns

As the day dawns
and light floods the sky,
may hope fill your mind
and love touch your life.

### May memories be filled with joy

May memories be filled with joy.
May this day be filled with peace.
May the future offer hope
of all we have yet to share,
as we travel on in life.

There are those who would not be comfortable with naming God in church or joining in worship with others, but who would claim that God does exist and that there is a spiritual dimension to their lives.

## God is the still centre of our lives

God is the still centre of our lives.
God is the source of quiet and peace for which we crave.
God is the listener, the gentle friend.
God is our reflection, a mirror to our true selves.
God is the warmth in our hearts, the co-creative mind.
God is love and will never leave us.

## May love be woven into the tapestry of the days

May love be woven into the tapestry of the days.
May the threads of joy and sorrow
create a pattern held together
by strands of compassion, care and companionship.
May all be held safe
in the frame of the love of God.

For those who find it difficult to name God for themselves, there are still blessings.

## May the days be filled with sunshine

May the days be filled with sunshine
even when clouds cover the earth.
May joy flood each moment
and laughter rattle the windows.
    May love dry the tears
    and tenderness soothe and heal.
    May the stars watch over us,
    and moonlight bathe our sleep.

### Let memories warm us

Let memories warm us
as we drift into sleep.
Let hope hearten us
as we wake to a new day.
Let life energize us
as we face its challenges.

### As the light fades

As the light fades
and darkness takes control,
may the flickering candle of hope
burn on through the night
until dawn's light
breaks through again.

And we end with a version of a very old and traditional blessing.

Simeon was an old man who worshipped in the temple in Jerusalem at the time of the birth of Jesus. He met Joseph and Mary and their child and recognized how important Jesus was and would be. Lk. 2.29–32 records a song that he sang in praise of Jesus which has been known in the church as the Nunc Dimittis. Simeon felt his life was complete after he had seen Jesus and so this blessing, inspired by his words, is a suitable conclusion to this collection:

**The end**
The end.
With everything complete.
No loose ends.
Blessed with every blessing
and every hope fulfilled.
This is our prayer.
Let us go in peace,
in the continuing enfolding love
of our neighbours
(and our God).
So be it (Amen).

# ALPHABETICAL INDEX OF FIRST LINES AND COPYRIGHTS

The items marked SB are © Stainer & Bell Ltd, P.O. Box 110. Victoria House, 23 Gruneisen Road, London N3 1DZ. Authors' copyrights are as follows: AP – Andrew Pratt; MD – Marjorie Dobson.

# THEMATIC INDEX